# *OrdinaryHeroes*

A TRIBUTE TO MEDAL OF HONOR RECIPIENTS:
REFLECTIONS OF FREEDOM, FAITH, DUTY AND THE HEROIC
POSSIBILITIES OF THE EVERYDAY HUMAN SPIRIT.

PHOTOGRAPHIC PORTRAITS, CAPTIONS AND EPILOGUE BY TOM CASALINI

STORY BY TIMOTHY WALLIS

© 2000 Tom Casalini
Published and distributed by Sweet Pea Press,
10-1/2 North Main Street, Zionsville, Indiana 46077
1-800-755-3706

No part of this book may be reproduced by any means
without the written permission of the publisher.

A portion of the proceeds from the sale of this book
goes to The Congressional Medal of Honor Society,
Charleston, S.C.

For more information about The Congressional Medal
of Honor Society and The Medal of Honor Recipients,
visit their website
at http://www.cmohs.org

Design: The Design Group, Inc., Indianapolis, Indiana
Printed in Italy

ISBN 0-9704410-0-2

Library of Congress Card Number: 00-192147

## Dedications

To my four children:
Guido, Eli, Liza, and Sophie –
that they will hold fast to the Spirit
and do their duty in their lives.

– Tom Casalini

To my parents who taught me
to find beauty in the ordinary things.
A rusty hinge. A grey day.
A cobweb. A neighbor.

– Timothy Wallis

Acknowledgments of gratitude
from Tom Casalini:

This project could not have the
life it has without those that touched it
along the way with their caring and
passion. My gratitude and love to:
My studio manager and keystone
Margie Janes for her countless hours,
dedication and insights; Chris Bucher,
my photographic assistant, for the
selfless giving of his talents; my
spiritual group buddies Tim and Mick
Fortner and Jeff Dupree for their
guidance and reminders of the lessons
learned along the way; The Design
Group team for their vision, passion
and respect for the book design and its
message; Indianapolis Photolab, for
their special care and consideration
of the photographs; my partner,
wife and friend Elizabeth for her
strength, love and encouragement at
every step; and the 48 men in this
book for the opportunity to learn the
"wonderfulness of ordinary."

## The Heroes.

"Ordinary Heroes" is about one of the most exclusive groups of men and women in the world — The Congressional Medal of Honor Recipients. Each member holds the nation's highest recognition for valor in combat.

Since The Medal was established in 1862, only 3,453 men and women have received it. Nineteen people have received this honor twice. To date, 2,386 Medals have been awarded to members of the Army; 745 to members of the Navy; 295 to members of the Marines; 16 to members of the Air Force; nine to unknown soldiers; and one to a member of the Coast Guard.

Forty-eight of the currently living Recipients have been interviewed and photographed for this book.

## The Citations.

Out of respect for these heroes, we have included their actual Medal of Honor Citations at the back of this book. Although we believe the citations are an important part of the complete story, many of the men are personally uncomfortable to have them read in public. They would rather be remembered for the hundreds of other accomplishments they have made in their lives — both the ordinary and the magnificent.

*I never woke up and went to war. I woke up and went to the sandbox. It seems to me that much of my generation grew up the same way. Fortunate. And, hopefully, very grateful.*

*The fact is, these men risked their lives to afford me mine. And so, this is the perspective I used in writing this story – a chronicle of my youth against these soldiers' sacrifices.*

*If you have ever been at a loss as to whom to thank for your freedom, or for the peace your children enjoy, you can start with these men. If you've never thought about it, I hope that, now, you will.*

Timothy Wallis

## The Hedge.

I was born between wars. In the belly of 1958. Amongst fields of heather I fondly recall mightily heaving a wadded parachute soldier into skies of cobalt and watching as the winds would carry it into enemy territory.

There were thickets of twisted briar, pillared oaks and magical mirrored ponds we weren't allowed to wade into. But most vivid in my memory is the yard of Mrs. Curr, an aging woman who bore no children and, at a distance, had a frightening resemblance to the Wicked Witch of the West. Up close it wasn't merely a resemblance. To me, she was indeed the witch. Right down to the wart with the hair sprouting out.

Separated by a hedge that couldn't grow fast enough for either of us, her yard was off limits. It was a land from which no child's toy ever returned. I can't recall how many times I watched a breeze lift my tiny plastic soldier just out of grasp and over that hedge, but I can tell you this. It drained the joy right out of me. It turned a day of laughter into hours of plotting. How was I going to have fun? How was I going to salvage the rest of my weekend? But most importantly, how was I going to slip through the hedge undetected, rescue my "parachute man" and make it back alive?

So there I was, a nine-year-old boy, seeing my world slip away as my camouflaged parachute disappeared behind that hedge.

What I wasn't able to comprehend at the time was that Major Leo Thorsness hung from the straps of his own parachute that very spring day. But there was no hedge. There were only the mountain ridges of North Vietnam and a whole forest swarming with enemy troops. Suddenly Mrs. Curr seemed a rather sweet old soul.

Flying his 93rd mission, the F-105 Major Thorsness piloted was ruptured by a MIG missile over the Pacific Ocean. At 675 mph he ejected. The relief of his chute opening was soon extinguished and the fear of where he was about to plummet crept into his blood. A fear that would quickly be hidden and replaced with stubborn perseverance as he became a prisoner of war. Whatever wild and wicked vision I had about the "other side of the hedge" could never compare to what was about to happen to Leo Thorsness in the craggy mountains of North Vietnam.

In an attempt to get information that would benefit the North Vietnamese, he was interrogated continuously. It was, in his words, "the routine of the prison."

Locked either in solitary confinement or in a cell with one or two other prisoners, he tried to survive his first three years in captivity. He soon came to understand the only answers they wanted were the ones that made them look good. If you didn't comply, you were harshly slapped off your stool and dragged and tugged by the roots of your hair. The tears would bead up in your eyes and the hate would coil up in your throat as you bit your tongue to keep from spewing out words that would guarantee you even more beatings.

The episodes were brutal and abundant. Your calendar was on your chest, shoulders and back. The days marked by gashes from the lashings and cruelty.

But what seems a bit odd about all of this is that Leo Thorsness didn't receive The Medal of Honor for being a prisoner of war. He received it for "conspicuous gallantry and intrepidity in action at the risk of his life above and beyond the call of duty." He received it for an incident in the clouds over North Vietnam. He received it while in the seat of his F-105 fighter jet still connected to civilization by a radio with an American voice on the other end and with the comfort of his finger on the trigger of a machine-gun that could spit a thousand rounds of ammunition a second.

But what about the six years he would endure in a Viet Cong prison camp? Stripped of his uniform, his weapons and his dignity, he was forced to emotionally die inside or endure. He chose to endure. For this, he deserves maybe another half-dozen medals. But medals aren't what Leo Thorsness is all about.

It's been said that character is what you do when no one is looking. Well, for six exhausting years no one looked at Major Thorsness, except his captors and a handful of other American POWs, and it is likely during this time he became the man of which he is most proud. Granted, he went on to serve in the United States Air Force and retire in the rank of Colonel and with that should come much pride. But somewhere between the heavy, humid suppression of the jungle and glances skyward beyond the razor wire, he gained a sense of humor, faithfulness and humility.

When asked what his thoughts are today upon seeing the American flag, his voice softens and he recounts the story of a fellow prisoner of war by the name of Mike Christian. Mike was a quiet, solitary man who was fiercely loyal to causes in which he believed. Old Glory was one of those causes and Mike was intent on making sure the prison camp had a flag. An American flag.

The North Vietnamese of course had severe consequences for any prisoner caught with an American flag. The beatings were barbaric. Yet Mike persisted. Time and time again he would be punished. And time and again he would begin anew, fashioning his flag.

Mike would scavenge grungy, tattered scraps of cloth and then, from the rubble of bricks, he would grind the bits and pieces into a

crimson powder that he used to stain the flag's seven red stripes. By smashing wet rice, he was able to formulate a type of glue that he used to paste the elements together. Stars were made of uniform buttons and Saint Christopher medals that he hung in a field of blue.

To witness what this man would go through as a prisoner of war was an amazing inspiration to Major Thorsness, who says he can still see his comrade huddled in the dark under his mosquito netting with a needle made from a bamboo splinter.

He would sit for hours in the thick, choking heat of this foreign purgatory and thread together an American flag. Beneath his bashed and bruised flesh was a spirit that refused to be tortured.

"When I see a flag flying I think of Mike Christian," says Thorsness. "He did it to keep his hopes up, and in the process he lifted everyone's beyond measure."

The Vietnam war ended and Leo Thorsness was finally able to go home. He returned to the person he admires most, his wife, and to that of which he is most proud, his family. "Wives always imagine the worst," he says. "She hung in there not knowing if I was alive or dead. Many marriages didn't last. Mine did, because of her."

What a spouse reads in the paper and hears on the news has got to be anguishing beyond words when their partner is off to war. But to have your letters returned unopened and marked "deceased" by the North Vietnamese would test even the most hopeful spirit. Being a father myself, I can only imagine being a prisoner of war with a child back home. Leo Thorsness' daughter was 11 years old when he was captured. When he saw her next, she was 18.

Upon having this sink in, I tried to picture many of the special moments they both missed sharing. Musicals. Science fairs. First date. First kiss. First time driving a car. And of course all the insignificant stuff in between that suddenly seems so very significant once you take it all away. He missed the blessing of seeing his daughter grow from a little girl into a young woman. He missed the blessing of time.

As my mind flashes back to those boyhood days of tossing parachute men into the blustery currents overhead, I will forever look at those times differently.

I will remember the fields of heather. The hedge. And, of course, Mrs. Curr. But I will also remember Leo Thorsness. The real parachute man. For it is because of him that I will never again take for granted one of this world's most overlooked gifts. The sweet randomness of being born between wars.

## The Hush.

A wisp of air tickles the peach fuzz on my seven-year-old legs as I lay napping on the daybed of our screened-in porch. In the rear room of my dreams, I am lullabied to sleep again by the lovely distant drone of a freight train making its way down to the muggy basin of the Ohio River for its cargo. It's just one of the sounds of my youth that has melted into my subconscious and become a present part of the quilt that I wrap around myself whenever the world seems too cold. But for those who went off to war, there are different sounds that play hide-and-seek amongst the lobes of their recollections.

"I can still hear them," Einar Ingman says of the bugles the Chinese used to signal their troops. The eerie blares that sliced through the blackness of nightfall and slipped up under your helmet and haunted you till dawn.

For some it's not so much the war in totality that sticks in their mind. It's a single moment — an image — an act. It's a remembrance of something that touches you or disturbs you for a lifetime. For Bob Modrzejewski, it was during a firefight one North Vietnamese night.

The sky was no longer the sky. It was a smoky orange and cherry shade lit up occasionally by flares dropped from friendly planes overhead for visibility. But as those flares dimmed and their embers fizzled to the ground, an ugly darkness enveloped the battlefield again. And between the enemy's whistles and the deafening artillery, you could hear the rustling and scraping of the North Vietnamese Army dragging their dead soldiers out of the fields all around you. Strange how such a hushed, obscure sound can still be the loudest noise in your head after three decades.

As tracers buzz and streak overhead, Carl Sitter moves from one foxhole to another checking on his men. He remembers the smell of death that can linger over a valley like an invisible fog. "People only see the parades and don't realize the cost of those Medals," says Sitter. "Many people did heroic deeds of valor greater than ours, but their witnesses had been killed or they were killed. We also tend to forget the everyday heroics of police and doctors and firefighters. The things

they do let others get on with a productive life. No medals are given for that. The things they do in Sunday school classes or in Boy Scouts. It's nothing really newsworthy. No one was shot or killed. But it's important stuff."

Receiving The Medal of Honor for Carl Sitter has meant an obligation to support our youth. He believes it's vital to "be there" and not just pull out our checkbooks, but to donate something more valuable — our time.

He recalls the person he most admires isn't a president or a general but his fifth grade teacher, Florence Givens. She came to his house to help him. To take him under her wing. She simply told him he could do better than he was doing. And so he did.

The moment that brings it all into perspective for Mike Fitzmaurice is a rather surreal one. It was Christmas Eve and his thoughts wanted to be somewhere warm — somewhere safe. But the task at hand was for him and six other soldiers to slip outside the wire of their camp and set up an ambush for the Viet Cong in a nearby graveyard.

With the cold rain dripping from the jungle vines overhead, he breathed on his fingertips to keep them thawed. It was so quiet that, in between the rain pellets smacking the broad leaves of the underbrush, you could hear your skin shiver. Then, off in the distance, was the muffled "thwack, thwack" of a helicopter. Its blades shoving the thick, damp, soupy air. As it drew closer and began to circle the base, Fitzmaurice heard a most amazing sound — music — Christmas music.

Playing out of loud speakers from the helicopter, the lyrics "peace on earth, good will toward men" drifted down into the jungle.

And suddenly, the night became warmer and the mist on his lips tasted more like wine. The chopper then turned and flew away, trailing the song with it into the hills. And the soldiers sat there in the graveyard of Vietnam waiting for the dawn of Christmas Day.

As I awoke that same Christmas morning to the softness of flannel and the smell of French toast, I had no knowledge of the seven soldiers keeping their dangerous vigil halfway around the globe. As I look back, I am grateful for what these men did for me. I am comforted somewhat in knowing that one night, many years ago, truly was a silent night.

## The Faith.

In a meadow, on my back, is where I spent much of my boyhood summer days. I would pull dandelions from the fields and blow their fluff up into the sky and watch as the winds would escort them into oblivion. I often wondered where they went. To other towns, other countries? Perhaps. But I always liked to think they went to heaven. Up where the angels would spin them into clouds. The very clouds I watched float past my window to the world. It's one of my earliest thoughts of godliness. Was there a god? Surely this world, this beauty around us, didn't just evolve. And if it did, from what did it evolve? And how did that come to be?

At some point we all have our faith tested. For many, it was in battle. When you're fighting for your very life, it's curious how you find faith. But some didn't have to look very far.

Van Barfoot was born in 1919. He fought in World War II and tells of the intense yet primitive training they were given. Stovepipes were used to simulate mortars, and sticks were held as makeshift rifles. He remembers the heavy water-cooled machine guns he actually carried through Italy. But he also carried something else with him — his faith. It began with his mother, who instilled in him a strong religious belief. She would hold his hand in church and he often felt that, as he marched across a battlefield, he was again holding her hand or the hand of his wife or sister. When they all three left this earth, he felt that their hands were replaced by the Lord's hand. And that is how he has lived his life. Holding on to his beliefs. The belief that everyone is your brother and that we need our fellow man. "I saw a lot of black and white men lying bleeding on the field of battle, and as far as I could tell, their blood was the same color," says Barfoot.

In Italy, he recalls the entire unit attending religious service. Catholics, Protestants and Jews would visit each other's services and listen. Before heading into battle one gloomy morning, Barfoot suggested reading the Bible aloud before departing. A fellow soldier lit a cigarette and Barfoot pulled the New Testament from his pocket. By the glow from the lighter's flame, he read three verses of Matthew to his congregation of Americans. They then marched off to war.

Michael Novosel is known as "The Last Eagle," a moniker that distinguishes him as the final pilot of World War II to retire from the military. He, too, believes that mankind is of one author. He states, "I have served my country with men of different religions. There were other Christians, Jews, Buddhists, Muhammadans and agnostics. They would not let me down, ever. Isn't that Christian, Jewish, Buddhist, Islamic of them."

Walter Ehlers, who lost his brother when the ship his brother was on was hit on D-Day, tells of a comrade who was under attack while with him in Africa. "The Germans were attacking and Pete was digging a foxhole. All the while he was screaming 'Oh God help me, oh God help me.' I later asked him after the shelling had stopped why he was asking God to help him since he was

an atheist? Pete replied, 'Well hell, there was no one else to ask'." It gives credence to the saying "there are no atheists in foxholes."

Most recipients of The Medal of Honor have citations that describe them brandishing weapons in their gallant efforts to save lives and advance their division's cause. However, the citation for Desmond T. Doss is absent of any action with him holding a gun. His beliefs prevented him from carrying a weapon of any kind. Even in war. He relied on his faith and his deep respect for the value of human life to get him through. As a medic, he believed in saving life, not taking it. And so Desmond Doss did just that. He saved lives.

In one intense battle on Okinawa, Doss helped treat the wounds of many men and, in the onslaught of heavy enemy fire, boldly lowered them down a jagged cliff to safety. During this action he was hit and, rather than put another medic's life in jeopardy, went about treating his own wound. Ironically, he strapped a shattered rifle stock to his fractured arm as a splint and crawled to an aid station using only his faith as ammunition.

These days, when I lie in a field, it is with my son on one side and my daughter on the other and they blow dandelion fluff into the air and they ask where it is that the seeds go. I tell them they are on their way to heaven where the angels spin them into clouds. They look at me and smile and have enough faith in me to believe that such a wonderful story is actually true.

And I have faith that they will remember it and treasure it enough to pass it on to their children.

## The Little Things.

It was a huge tree. I'm not really sure how big, but big! Of course, when you're eight years old most trees look big. I'm not even sure what kind it was. An oak. Beech maybe. What I do remember is that I liked to climb it.

That tree was my home for an entire summer. We would ascend its branches with precision and grace, but the challenge and excitement came in getting down. It became a game to see how fast we could get from the top of its crown to the ground without breaking ours. We would time each other by watching the second hand sweep around the faces on our little Timex® watches. As we gained confidence in our ability, we would grab every other branch on our descent so as not to slow us down. By the end of the summer, we could flash through the inner sanctuary of that 80-foot tree in about four-and-a-half seconds, grabbing only three or so limbs just long enough to slow us without scrubbing off too much crucial speed.

On the drop down, all you could see were splinters of sunlight flashing through the canopy of leaves and then an abrupt billow of dust as your Red Ball Jets slapped the earth below. What a memory. Testament to the fact that it's the little things that will forever be more memorable than the monumental things in life.

It's what's harvested between the lines of The Medal of Honor citations that hold as much of the story of these men as the battles they fought.

Barney Barnum says of putting war in perspective, "It's about the things one marine does for another marine. You don't do it for the flag or for motherhood. You do it so as not to let your buddy down. It's about the person on your right or your left."

He talks about his time in Vietnam and the moments that don't make the headlines but are at the core of success, survival and sanity. "It's sharing from a canteen, cutting your last cigarette in half, helping carry a guy's machine-gun who is exhausted," he says. "War stories don't need to be talked about. If you were there and saw the killing and destruction, that's enough. It's not cocktail stuff.

"Humor is important," continues Barnum. "You gotta laugh and not take yourself too serious."

When he was on the gun loop, which was six guys with wire communications acting as lookouts, he said the joviality and camaraderie were incredible.

In the darkness of Nam they would sit clutching their machine-guns and share stories of football and girls. It was like laughing in the back of church. You were about to split a gut, but knew how dangerous that could be.

Of all the situations he was in while at war, Howard Lee most vividly remembers holding a kid in his arms who was dying. He looked the boy in the face and it struck him how young he was. "He was actually 18 or so but looked 14. It shook me. The sum of what the sacrifice was for him. It was so sad. Here was this kid in the flower of his manhood struck down."

The finality and loneliness of "Taps" is what really gets to Francis Currey. "It's a very emotional thing for me," Currey says, whose platoon leader was killed at Royal River Crossing in Belgium. Whenever he returns there, he makes a point to stop at the cemetery.

Charles Murray thinks a lot about his platoon. "That's what the war is to you. Your small group of eight to 10 guys," says Murray. "You hold their hands while they die. That's what I think about."

Six years after the battle in which Murray was cited for The Medal of Honor, he visited the actual area with his wife and his sons who were ages four and six. Among random ammo boxes and sporadic shell casings, his mind flipped back to the bitter cold battle when a German soldier tossed the grenade that wounded him. He tries to visualize why he was spared and others died as bullets ripped at his boots and clothes and yet never took his life. And then he sees his sons fishing in a nearby pond that he once marched past as a First Lieutenant and wonders if he's looking at the answer.

## The Dark.

The tiptop of the river birch trees began to hush as the night sifted down into the meadow. A choir of crickets started and I remember how I loved just being a boy in my backyard. All around me, flashes of yellow-gold as the fireflies danced from out of the woods and into the open. Hundreds of tiny lanterns glowing and then vanishing as I trundled after them holding my clear jar and its tin lid I'd poked with an ice pick. Reaching and grabbing the gentle creatures, I would stuff them into my glass bank. And, as the night came to a close, I would sit amongst the symphony cradling my treasure of lightning bugs, their beacons illuminating the sleepy smile that I wore wearily like a badge.

The darkness holds a different memory for Sammy Davis, who was at Firebase Cudgil in Vietnam. On a November night in 1967, Davis initiated a series of actions that earned him The Medal of Honor. Though compelling and diplomatic, his citation doesn't convey the emotions behind his duty. Here, some of Davis' own words help put some humanity to the harshness.

Forty-two men went on the assignment. In the end, 12 were left standing. "What I did that night was not bravery," states Davis, "it was determination. There is a difference."

It was 2:00 a.m. when the enemy's bugles and whistles signaled the beginning of chaos. Just to instill fear and confusion into the teenage American soldiers, the Vietnamese officers shouted their orders in English. They were so close you could hear the metal mortar shell casings sliding and grating down the steel launching tubes just before they were fired. Then hell became commonplace.

Davis' cannon was hit by a mortar shell, which knocked him into a foxhole. His leg wound felt like he was covered with fire ants, as sandbags exploded around him and bullets tore at the air about his head. The enemy was so near that he could hear them swimming across the river directly toward him. He fired his M-16 until it was out of ammunition, and then he blasted his M-60 machine-gun till it, too, was left empty and smoking.

Thinking he was the only American alive, he sat in the unlit forest and felt for pellets of gunpowder that had spilled onto the ground, which he desperately needed to fire the howitzer. He packed it to maximum charge and counted the clicks in the dark to set the timed fuse to muzzle action. This would turn the howitzer into a shotgun and shoot a beehive of 18,000 darts in a single round. He mashed and twisted the massive cannon into position by himself and fired. It lurched and recoiled on its trail, falling on Davis and crushing his ribs.

Then, out of the blindness from across the river, a voice: "Don't shoot. I'm a GI." An American or another Vietnamese ploy? Davis then saw the man was black, assuring himself it was no trick. Once on the other river bank, he found two more wounded soldiers. One missing a foot and the other having been shot through one ear and out the other.

Although he thought the soldier was dead, Davis refused to leave him behind and swam all three across the river to safety.

But the hardest part of the battle was the next morning.

"You see your friends lying dead and it makes you so hollow inside," recalls Davis. "You kneel next to a dead buddy and realize how much you loved that guy. You knew his girlfriend's name and what he did on his first date. He's lying there with his eyes open and blood splattered on his face. You're there on your knees getting the mud out of his mouth because you don't want anyone to see him this way. It breaks your heart."

As the day sneaks once again into evening, Davis sees a three-year-old Vietnamese girl wandering amongst the shredded buildings and smoldering rubble holding a two-gallon bucket and filling it with chunks of brick.

He asks a nearby village woman if she knows the girl and what she is doing. He is told that her parents have been killed, she has no other family and she is on her own. To earn her way, she gathers bits and pieces of brick from the devastation. She then tugs and drags her bucket down to where they make cement and sells the fragments for pennies. This is what she uses to buy food.

Davis looked across the way at this soft, sweet child holding her bucket of rubble as though it were gold. She turned and disappeared down a road, all alone in the world at the age of three. As flashes of yellow-gold exploded all around her, I can't help but think how different our lives were. And yet how the same they were. Separated only by longitudes and latitudes and the politics in between.

With all The Medal of Honor Recipients, I ended by saying, "What's the most important question I didn't ask?" "Well," said Davis, "there is one question you didn't ask. You didn't ask if it was worth the trip." And so I asked, "Was it worth the trip?" He responded by saying, "It was worth a thousand trips."

And then he tells me the story of the man who he swam to safety, the soldier that had been shot through the head. The one he thought was dead, the one he had refused to leave behind.

He had lived. And Davis saw him many years after the war. The soldier introduced Davis to the son he was able to conceive after returning from Vietnam.

And then the soldier's son handed Davis his baby daughter to

hold. "If I had not done my job that night long ago, that soldier's precious little granddaughter would not have been in my arms. That's awesome. It overwhelmed me," said Davis. As it did me. And I thanked him for making the trip.

## The Hill.

Slivers of a sinking sun are taken hostage by the horizon as 12-year-olds race for a tent floating like an island in the yard. They pour inside the flap, giggling as the orbit of the earth envelops shadows from their rapid footsteps. And the dark little bubble of their safe domain is now lit by a domino of flashlights clicking on and then twirling and arcing like the electric charge of a neutron.

These are my memories of Indian summer evenings, being lured

into our sleeping bags by chill and slumber. It is here, at the edge of nightfall, that I feel most at home. Where I can summon a fond recollection and have a séance with my mind's souvenirs.

We would wake the following morning with our flashlights still switched on and clutched in our hands. The beam invisible in the blush of daybreak and the dim glow from the tiny, tired bulb softly warming our palms.

On the flip side of the atlas stood Jon Cavaiani, one of the soldiers who allowed me the luxury of my childhood. He defended my country along with other soldiers, marines and pilots who are now either fallen, frail or forgotten.

Cavaiani was born in England and grew up in Italy. In 1968 he got his U.S. citizenship, and in 1969 he enlisted in the United States Army and boarded a bus to Fort Ord. In the blink of three years he was in the middle of Vietnam as part of SOG, Studies and Observations Group. This code name represented the most elite and secret military unit to serve in the Vietnam War. It consisted of members of the Navy Seals, the Air Force Commandos and the Army Green Berets. All volunteers. And all so secret that the U.S. Government denied their very existence.

Hickory Hill, pockmarked and smoldering from relentless enemy fire, rose as a birthmark of American resistance and sacrifice. Surrounded by the North Vietnamese Army, the closest "friendlies" were 20 miles or so to the east at Firebase Fuller and Caroll. What made Outpost Hickory Hill so important to Americans wasn't just that it was a radio relay site, but also a secret National Security Agency radio monitoring post that used state-of-the-art automated technology to intercept enemy radio broadcasts. This is also what made it an important target for the North Vietnamese Army.

What happened on Hickory Hill earned Jon Cavaiani The Medal of Honor, but it came at a price that few, if any, would ever want to pay. Despite being outranked, the site was commanded by Cavaiani. He was assisted by Sergeant John Jones. This vital piece of land was only 29 yards wide and 73 yards long, and was held by 27 U.S. and 67 South Vietnamese soldiers.

The Hill's most intense assault came on June 4 and 5, 1971. A barrage of machine-gun fire, grenades, claymore mines and mortars began to take their toll on the small, diminishing American defenses. The situation seemed hopeless and Cavaiani called for an evacuation.

Helicopters came in and took many of the men out while Cavaiani, Jones and others stayed back to destroy the NSA top secret radio intercept equipment and to get gear to put on the next chopper. That's when Cavaiani learned the next chopper was also to be the last chopper. Each helicopter held seven men. Yet there were 28 still on Hickory Hill.

Hope brightened as he heard an Air Force "jolly green" was flying in to get the rest of the men. But seven miles out the pilot radioed saying that he would be court-martialed if he didn't turn around. He turned around.

Cavaiani and his men were stranded, the result of a bureaucratic squabble by an officer who didn't think much of SOG and its unconventional warfare.

The skies over Hickory Hill now were void of rescue helicopters and grew dark and desperate. The North Vietnamese were crawling up all sides of the hill like cockroaches toward table scraps. You couldn't see them as the heavens grew blacker and blacker, but you knew they were there. Cavaiani and his men quickly emptied a huge outhouse tub of its excrement and cut a hole for a machine-gun. He set up crossfire positions on either side of the helipad and then he perched himself atop a bunker.

A fog as thick as molasses oozed over Hickory Hill. The North Vietnamese attacked without hesitation. Muzzles flashed from the American crossfire and the enemy fell. Eight more waves of NVA attempted to reach the helipad, and eight more times they were gunned down. About 120 North Vietnamese lost their lives in a mere handful of minutes. Then silence.

Thinking the NVA was about to mount an all-out attack, Cavaiani deployed his troops into the heaviest bunkers. But as they were shifting positions, dozens of enemy rushed the helipad. Atop a bunker, Cavaiani sprayed ammunition at the approaching Vietnamese. But a slug hit him in the small of his back and tore all the way up into his shoulder. He rolled into a bunker with Jones and radioed to a Stinger helicopter that 100 enemy troops were out and in the open and to commence a gun run, stating that all his men were under cover. He gave his initials indicating that he accepted full responsibility for the fire mission. But fearing friendly casualties the pilot declined. The NVA was now tossing grenades into every bunker they could find as the Stinger could be heard retreating from the skies over Hickory Hill.

As two NVA soldiers creep through the doorway of the bunker, Cavaiani grabs the first one by the hair and, in a single adrenaline-filled heartbeat, thrusts his knife up through his chin, killing him. Jones shoots the second invader, who rolls out of the bunker but manages to toss in a grenade that explodes and severely injures Jones. Stumbling to his feet, Jones climbs out of the bunker to surrender. A gunshot rings out and Jones' dead body crashes back into the bunker. A second grenade bounces in after him. It explodes and knocks Cavaiani unconscious and destroys his radio.

He awoke to the dark, mustiness of the bunker being filleted by the beams of enemy flashlights. Their boots crunched in the rubble all about him. He felt the warmth of a fresh leg wound, and blood trickled from his eardrums and pooled in his ears. Playing dead, he locked his eyes open and unblinking, as the NVA's flashlights found him. A Vietnamese soldier then poked the barrel of his AK into his chest and ribs. Convinced Cavaiani was dead, he then took a cigarette lighter and lit the tarpaper roof of the bunker. As the enemy clamored out of the hideaway, hot tar from the blazing paper overhead dripped onto Cavaiani's face and the leg of his fatigues caught fire. Half buried beneath the collapsed bunker, he couldn't move to surprise the enemy, so he had to lie still in unbearable pain, smelling his flesh burn, until the two NVA soldiers walked away.

As Cavaiani finally struggled to the bunker's door, a bullet from a burning machine-gun ignited and grazed his head, again knocking him unconscious. This time, when he awoke, he was outside the burned-out bunker under a midnight sky where the only sounds were of looting and loneliness.

As an NVA soldier foraged next to him, Cavaiani reached for his remaining knife and pierced the enemy's breast plate with such force he couldn't pull the dagger back out. He left it pummeled into the man's chest with peeled pieces of his own seared skin still stuck to the handle.

As dawn began to break, Cavaiani managed to slink down a cliff face and headed toward the east in search of Firebase Fuller, which in the eyes of the U.S. Government didn't exist. Ten days of survival found Cavaiani just outside the wire of the base at 3:00 a.m. Before approaching it, he decided to sleep.

As he groggily stood up, a frail old man shoved a rifle in his back and five other communists descended from the surrounding jungle. Jon Cavaiani had just become a prisoner of war.

The prison camps were no reprieve from the brutality of war. He was beaten severely. In search of information regarding the National Security Agency's efforts on Hickory Hill, they crushed his ribs and broke his hand and spine. He went to Vietnam weighing 197 pounds and standing five feet, 10 inches tall. When he left, he weighed 90 pounds and stood five feet, seven-and-a-half inches.

While all the atrocities of combat and confinement chipped away at Jon Cavaiani, nothing was more devastating than what happened before he even set foot on Hickory Hill.

Jon Cavaiani arrived in Vietnam. During his first combat, the Sergeant Major that commanded his battalion was killed. Cavaiani compassionately adopted his slain commander's young Vietnamese son and proceeded to build an orphanage for other children who had lost their families through the ugly reality of war. Within a short time, the orphanage had grown to take in 37 children and seven monks who helped look after the kids.

Their playground, beneath a canopy of constantly exploding mortar shells, was so different from mine that it's difficult to conjure up where they could find joy. But the hearts of children are shields of strength and telescopes in search of happiness.

They found fun in the eyes of their playmates and in the innocence of their years. Then, one day, the laughter was snuffed out as the North Vietnamese Army besieged the orphanage, killing every child and breathing being in its path.

The sadness sank into Jon Cavaiani like a cancer. And, while he went on to valiantly defend America on Hickory Hill, survive as a POW and receive The Medal of Honor, he had yet to face his toughest battle.

In talking about his Posttraumatic Stress Disorder, Cavaiani sighs and says that he "brought too much home." I view it differently. I believe that he brought just enough home. He brought himself.

## The Twilight's Last Gleaming.

The twilight. It's that magic moment of light that hangs on the horizon just long enough to make us look at the day we spent in a different way. It gives us hope that the darkness which follows will be safe and that dawn's early light will find us.

It is in the twilight's last gleaming that I harbor some of my favorite childhood memories. Tossing my parachute man. Falling asleep on the screened porch. Blowing dandelion fluff toward heaven. Climbing towering trees. Chasing fireflies. And following flashlight beams out of a darkening woods.

It is also in the twilight, as I now watch my own children play, that I realize what all the members of our armed forces did for me. And are doing for me. My gratitude is eternal.

The chances of you meeting the men in this book are remote. The chances of you repaying them for their actions are even more remote. They have received The Medal of Honor. As a result, we, as individuals and as a nation, have received much more.

But the truly wonderful thing about these men is that they do not want to be repaid. Unless that payment comes in the form of living lives that are honest, fruitful and loyal. Maybe that's because these are just a few of the attributes that go into making a country free and making a person whole. Or maybe that's because these are some of the values for which many fought and for which many died.

Should you still not know why The Medal of Honor is bestowed upon an individual, I'd like to suggest you begin reading a few of the citations starting on page 131.

What you will find there are the actual words that describe the actions that warranted the highest medal in our land. And if you read between the lines, you will find men driven by the simple beauty of "doing their job."

These aren't men who want to be put on pedestals. You may find them at the gas station or next to you in the checkout lane of the supermarket. They are quietly leading lives by example, even with the burden of their own faults.

What makes them heroes isn't just the fact that they crawled on their bellies under a blaze of bullets and through a curtain of napalm to save a wounded soldier. It's that they also cared enough to discipline their children, to be faithful to their families and to be respectful of their fellow human beings.

These all take courage. And courage is something we find in facing our fears. In pursuing our dreams. Courage is what transforms ordinary men into heroes. It is what we find in the twilight's last gleaming.

*You are invited to take a journey of
freedom, faith, courage and duty.*

*Let yourself be drawn
into the experiences of these men.*

*Travel into their souls – your soul – and
return with a renewed vision of the wonderfulness and
strength of "ordinary" people.*

"I felt the hands of my mother, sister, and wife every time I went into combat. Now, after they have passed on, I feel their hands have been replaced by the hand of God."

*Van T. Barfoot*

U.S. ARMY, W.W. II

"It's about the things one marine does for another marine, sharing from a canteen, cutting your last cigarette in half, helping carry a guy's machine-gun when he is exhausted. You do it so as not to let your buddy down. It's about the man on your right or your left. I'm not a winner of The Medal of Honor. I'm a guardian of it...the keeper of The Medal of Honor."

*Harvey C. Barnum, Jr.*
U.S. MARINE CORPS, VIETNAM

"I volunteered for the paratroopers because my girlfriend back home asked if I would write her a letter on the way down. That was the lady I married 50 years ago."

Melvin E. Biddle

U.S. ARMY, W.W. II

He has 118 fragments in his
midsection, 18 in his head, and
12 in his right hand. He says,
"What is, is. Fear is time- and
mind-consuming and wasteful.
Fear may be contagious. Fear
does not spark superior endeavor,
but leads to inferior performance."

*James M. Burt*

U.S. ARMY, W.W. II

The greatest love of his life was his wife. She passed on a year before this photograph was taken. He's sitting on their love seat, surrounded by her favorite fabric.

*Robert Eugene Bush*

U.S. NAVAL RESERVE, W.W. II

The bond we witnessed between
him and his wife was exceptional.
The memories, flashbacks, and night
sweats that return with a soldier
from war become his partners as
well. She walked that unknowing
valley with him — with patience,
understanding and faith. They
walked it together. They walked it
straight into love.

*Jon R. Cavaiani*

U.S. ARMY, VIETNAM

He sat with his huge hands crossed
underneath his chin. His eyes looked
out to the horizon of his Oklahoma
homeland. The pride of a Native
American Indian, the pride of an
American soldier. "Chief Childers" is
a title bestowed upon him by
President Dwight D. Eisenhower.
Ironically, the symbol which came to
represent all that he fought against
in the war – the swastika –
was identical to his native peoples'
sign for peace, which he continues
to wear proudly today.

*Ernest Childers*

U.S. ARMY, W.W. II

"My prayers and faith in God gave
me the strength to face each moment
out on that battlefield, and my
desire for freedom for self and for my
country kept me going. When
Harry S. Truman presented me with
The Medal of Honor, he made the
statement that he would rather have
The Medal of Honor than be the
President of the United States."

*John R. Crews*

U.S. ARMY, W.W. II

President Dwight D. Eisenhower
personally told him that if his actions
had not taken place that day, the
war in Europe would have lasted six
more weeks.

*Francis S. Currey*

U.S. ARMY, W.W. II

His house is a four-column, two-story southern colonial. The massive size of the columns seem to match his accomplishments. He served in W.W. II, Korea and Vietnam. When he retired, he was Assistant Commandant of the Marine Corps, appointed by the President. His life is now filled with grandchildren, renewing his youth. He is proud of his contributions to the world in which his grandchildren now play.

*Raymond G. Davis*
U.S. MARINE CORPS, KOREA

One of his greatest joys in life today is the look on his granddaughter's face when she pulls that fish out of the pond.

Sammy L. Davis
U.S. ARMY, VIETNAM

When it came time to make his portrait he said, "Would you mind if we pray together for God's guidance?" In our short silent prayers together there was a oneness, a brotherhood.

*Desmond T. Doss*

CONSCIENTIOUS OBJECTOR, SEVENTH-DAY ADVENTIST
U.S. ARMY, W.W. II

The drive to his house was down a long country road in Illinois. It felt as if we were on a drive to meet my grandfather. His dog met us in the driveway. We were greeted at the door by his wife and daughter.
In our time together, we talked of the harvest of winter wheat and of planting the spring garden.

Russell E. Dunham

U.S. Army, W.W. II

On the 50th anniversary of D-Day at Normandy, he was a featured speaker in the ceremonies, along with the President and other heads of state. He fought the battle, and then stood on the same soil, with rushing memories, delivering words of strength and freedom.

Walter D. Ehlers

U.S. ARMY, W.W. II

He is the oldest living Medal of
Honor Recipient (90 at the time of
this photograph) and the last from
Pearl Harbor. His wife had recently
passed on, and he was happy to have
the company. It was the Saturday
before Easter Sunday and he invited
us to spend the night with him.
He talked of the day for which his
citation was written: He was leaving
the base driving his new Ford
pickup truck when he heard aircraft
overhead and saw the symbol
of the "rising sun" on their wings.
He turned his pickup around;
the rest is history. He still owns
the truck.

*John William Finn*

U.S. NAVY, W.W. II

At a Veterans' Administration Center in South Dakota, there is a display of awards, photographs and moving stories of one particular Medal of Honor Recipient. As people go through the center and view the display, they are curious if the man is still alive. The reply is, "Not only is he still alive, but he's right down the hall." The center is named after Michael Fitzmaurice, and he is a maintenance engineer there. A quiet, humble, gentle man leading an ordinary life.

*Michael John Fitzmaurice*

U.S. ARMY, VIETNAM

He told us how he was involved with
exposing a judge in the Chicago
area who had been posing as a
Medal of Honor Recipient for years,
and the events that took place
when the judge was confronted as
an impostor. How does someone
pretend to have lived through
the darkness of war? There was
disdain in his eyes as he told us the
story. He was defending integrity,
honor and respect.

*Harold A. Fritz*

U.S. ARMY, VIETNAM

He is now a computer programmer
building computer simulations for
Army Strategy Training. In the
computer world, the terrain,
weather, movements of troops and
equipment are all preprogrammed,
so operations can be viewed in
real time with real potential effects.
Yet could the clicks of his mouse
ever be as "real" as his memories of
being a medic in Vietnam?

*Charles Chris Hagemeister*

U.S. ARMY, VIETNAM

He was an inspiration. It was difficult for him to speak. With few words, he gave us a great deal.

*Rodolfo P. Hernandez*
U.S. ARMY, KOREA

He was recovering from yet
another back operation. A plaguing
injury from his last parachute
jump in Vietnam. When he walked
around the corner in his civilian
clothes, one could only imagine him
in full military dress. His shirt
was neatly tucked, his pants
razor-creased, his shoes spotless.
His discipline unwavering. I wanted
to snap to a salute.

Robert L. Howard

U.S. Army, Vietnam

"My seven children are my life's greatest joy. I leave them a heritage of love, of God, of honesty and love of country. Fear knocks on your door. Faith answers. No one is there."

Einar H. Ingman, Jr.
U.S. ARMY, KOREA

When we arrived at his home, he met us out in his front yard. It was difficult and emotional for him when he thought of his time spent in Vietnam. We stayed in the yard, not wanting to intrude any further.

Leonard B. Keller

U.S. ARMY, VIETNAM

One can never tell by looking at a
man the things that may be harbored
within his soul.

*Howard V. Lee*

U.S. Marine Corps, Vietnam

He's the kind of guy you could drink
a six-pack of beer and exchange
fishing stories with all afternoon.

*Gary Lee Littrell*
U.S. ARMY, VIETNAM

We had been told that there was no way we could photograph him without his Texas cowboy hat. On oxygen and struggling to get around, he asked to be photographed outdoors. He removed his oxygen tube from his nose and we helped him outside. His inner strength was strong, his eyes determined.

James M. Logan
U.S. ARMY, W.W. II

Some things are kept inside a man.

Some things are never spoken.

They are only seen in his eyes.

*Allen James Lynch*

U.S. ARMY, VIETNAM

He is a mountain of a man; facing
the challenges of being a single
father with two teenage children;
challenged with the memories
of Vietnam.

Franklin D. Miller

U.S. ARMY, VIETNAM

He was surrounded by a whole life
lived in the military, and gracious
enough to share it with two men who
never served.

*Lewis L. Millett*

He is very involved with his church,
and seems to approach his worship
with all the dedication of a marine.

*Robert J. Modrzejewski*
U.S. MARINE CORPS, VIETNAM

He is a quiet man, no bigger than a minute. Very few words were spoken during our visit. The presence of his silence was more powerful than words.

*Jack C. Montgomery*

"What he is about to tell you," Mrs. Murray continued, "is that he was with that man, holding his hand when he died." Charles Murray had been talking about a young man named Lombardi who had been looking for information about his father, killed in W.W. II. Lombardi's mother was so distraught at her husband's death that she destroyed all the physical memories of him, and the boy had grown up knowing nothing about him. After his mother passed on, he went in search of his father, and his journey brought him to Murray. Ironically, the last eyes his father had looked into were Murray's. And, when young Lombardi also looked into Charles Murray's eyes, I believe he found all the fatherly strength, love and compassion for which he had been searching.

*Charles P. Murray, Jr.*
U.S. ARMY, W.W. II

"I felt that whatever I did, I had to be a credit to the Marine Corps. Once a marine, always a marine. We had to succeed. When the 5th and 7th returned from battle with all their equipment, carrying their dead with them, marching into our company, they broke into the Marine Corps Hymn. I had tears in my eyes and I will never forget that moment."

*Reginald R. Myers*

U.S. MARINE CORPS, KOREA

He is the "Last Eagle," the last
W.W. II pilot to retire. His Medal of
Honor citation is from Vietnam.

*Michael J. Novosel*

U.S. ARMY, VIETNAM

He's a tough, wiry fellow with a
New York accent in the middle of
Texas and he loves it. In the log
cabin that he and his wife designed
and built, she does her art work
and he enjoys the solitude of being.

Robert E. O'Malley

U.S. Marine Corps, Vietnam

He is the watch dog; guardian of
the integrity of The Medal of Honor.
He has tracked down hundreds of
Medal of Honor impostors. He begins
his California day at 5:00 a.m.
"because that's when it is 8:00 a.m.
in Washington, D.C., and my FBI
agent is in his office." (There is an
FBI agent working with him to
expose Medal of Honor impostors.)
He is in his 80s, still doing his
duty for his fellow man; holding
honesty, honor and country first
and foremost.

*Mitchell Paige*
U.S. MARINE CORPS, W.W. II

He works for the VA helping
soldiers who are ready for discharge
to understand their benefits
due them by the U.S. Government.
Still helping to protect his
fellow comrades.

Robert Martin Patterson

U.S. ARMY, VIETNAM

He is a man who is now very relaxed
and happy. Proud to be a father.
Proud of his children.

*Richard A. Pittman*

U.S. MARINE CORPS, VIETNAM

"I have tried not to let The Medal of Honor affect my life. But the memories will always be with me."

Everett Parker Pope
U.S. MARINE CORPS, W.W. II

The walls he has built around
himself were difficult to scale. But
there is an understanding that takes
place, sometimes, just by touching
the wall.

Ronald Eric Ray

U.S. ARMY, VIETNAM

He loves driving his antique
panel truck to work everyday. He
works with veterans, helping them
confront the problems that come
with Posttraumatic Stress Disorder.

*Louis R. Rocco*

"I did it because I would have been
ashamed not to have." He followed
his fallen brother to Korea; not
to avenge his brother's death, but to
simply take his place.

Ronald E. Rosser

U.S. ARMY, KOREA

He was studying for his Master's
Degree in Theology so he could go
out into the community and be of
assistance to the elderly in his church
who are unable to attend services.
He passed away on April 4, 2000,
before his desire of continuing to do
his duty on earth could be fulfilled.

Carl L. Sitter

U.S. Marine Corps, Korea

Jim Swett had driven six hours one way to meet us at Jim Taylor's house. The two Jims have been friends for over 25 years, celebrating holidays together with their families. When we arrived, there was a soft-topped Jeep in the driveway with a license plate that read, "Sit down, shut up and pour me a Dickle." It belonged to Jim Swett. It was like sitting with two of our own old buddies talking about hunting, fishing, families and other fun things in life. The two men teased and joked with one another, and it was beautiful to witness their

*continued on next page*

*James Elms Swett*

U.S. MARINE CORPS RESERVE, W.W. II

*continued from previous page*

quiet expression of brotherly love.
Jim Taylor talked about selling his
home one day and moving to
northern California to be closer to
Jim Swett. Two vets: one of W.W. II,
the other of Vietnam. Two different
men sharing one common thread:
the love for life and their families.
It was difficult to leave these men;
their kindness towards us was
overwhelming. We left with a feeling
of gratitude for their contributions
to this world that allow us to
build our own homes for our own
loving families.

*James Allen Taylor*

U.S. ARMY, VIETNAM

He is affectionately referred to by
his fellow Medal of Honor Recipients
as "Big Mike." I had gotten a peek
at his personality from John Finn.
The story goes that, toward the end
of her life, John's wife was confined
to a wheelchair. They were at a
Medal of Honor social function and
Mrs. Finn wanted very much to
dance. Dancing had been a love of
her life. Upon hearing about it,
"Big Mike" grabbed a tablecloth,
fashioned a sling out of it, lifted
her out of her wheelchair, and
put her into the sling. She danced
her last dance with "Big Mike."
A man as big in compassion as he is
in stature.

*Michael Edwin Thornton*

U.S. NAVY, VIETNAM

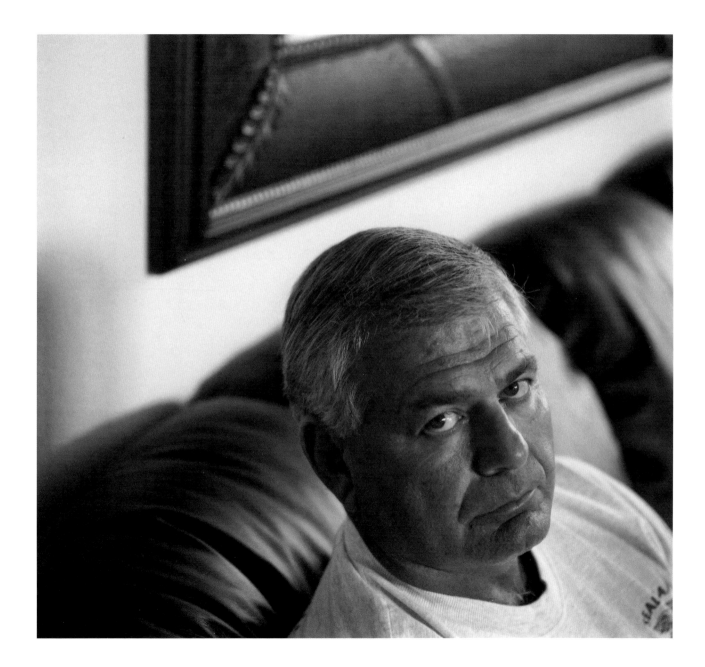

"It wasn't The Medal that changed my life. It was being a prisoner of war for six years."

Leo K. Thorsness

U.S. Air Force, Vietnam

When he answered the door, he
had just finished vacuuming the
house for his fiancée Dawn. He is
a free spirit, a man's man, who loves
to ride his Harley® and feel the
freedom of the wind. In years past,
he was the leader of a Harley
motorcycle club. He told us of an
event one day when an angry young
man wanted to burn an American
flag. "Why don't you start with this
one," he said as he pointed to the
flag that was sewn to his jacket.
Always on duty, he never forgets the
cost or the symbol of freedom.

*Gary George Wetzel*
U.S. ARMY, VIETNAM

"I entered the service when I was 16 years old. I had three reasons: I had just finished the 9th grade and didn't want to go back to school the next year; I wanted to get away from home and go out on my own; and I really liked the looks of the Navy uniform and had read a great deal about the travel and adventure of the Navy."

He is the most decorated man in the history of the United States Navy.

James E. Williams

U.S. NAVY, VIETNAM

*M*ost of my life, my photographs have
spoken for me. I communicate through
the lens of a camera. This book is no exception.

I wanted you to see these men as I saw them.
To learn about their experiences, their thoughts
and their lives, just as I did.

Now, I would like to share the personal journey I have
taken during the development of this book. It was
a journey of miles and meetings with strangers who
became brothers. And it was also about long-ago
memories and the love of family.

The most important part of this Epilogue, however,
is the message I have been entrusted to deliver to you on
behalf of these men...these Ordinary Heroes.

Tom Casalini

## Memories.

My first memories of a soldier were overheard conversations. They took place in the early 1950s, between my mother and her siblings, about the loss of their brother, my Uncle Ernie, in W.W. II. I was only seven at the time, and I had no real idea of the meaning of the conversations, but I could recognize the emotions. I figured my mother named my older brother in honor of her brother.

I grew up in a large Italian family. I have three older brothers and three older sisters. We lived in a typical neighborhood one block from school and church. Sunday mornings were a treat. My dad insisted that we all go to church together as a family. After the last mass of the morning, aunts, uncles, cousins and the parish priest would come to our house for brunch. The adults would talk, mostly in Italian, and we kids would eat and play.

My Aunt Ray and Uncle Ralph were two great people. They never had children of their own, so when we went out with them, the pocketbook opened endlessly. My Aunt Ray always had a smile on her face, a very positive and loving lady. My Uncle Ralph was a nervous man. He seemed to tap his foot constantly. He became my second contact with a soldier, only this one was real to me. I remember asking my father once why Uncle Ralph tapped his foot all the time. He simply answered "because of the war." I had no idea what that meant.

## An Insight.

One spring, the rains were heavy and parts of the town flooded. The water was over our back door steps and rising. My mother and father thought it would be best if we children went to stay with aunts and uncles in the country until the water subsided. My brother Ernie and I got to move in with Aunt Ray and Uncle Ralph. It was a mixed blessing for me because, although they were my favorite aunt and uncle, I was used to my own bed and my own lights being on. I was afraid of the dark.

During our stay, my brother went to a party one night and it was getting close to bedtime. I was stalling, because no way was I going to sleep in the dark alone. My Aunt Ray picked up on my stall tactics and was gracious enough to offer to make me a bedtime snack, giving me more time. While she was cooking, Uncle Ralph and I sat at the table together. He looked at me and said, "You are frightened, aren't you? You are scared of something. You don't have to answer me; I know. I've seen fear in eyes before, during the war. It's something I'll never forget." That was the first conversation I had with a war veteran, albeit a one-sided one. But it opened a window to an unknown world that I would visit years later.

## A Different Kind of Prisoner of War.

One day when I was in college, my mother phoned to relay some tragic news. Uncle Ralph had shot Aunt Ray several times with a handgun. Through an act of God, she survived. When I went home to visit her, I asked her to tell me the incidents that brought Uncle Ralph to shoot her. She said, "Tommy, we were just sitting watching T.V. and talking. The next thing I knew, your uncle got up and said, 'It's time to fight.' I had become the enemy in his eyes. Try to understand, Tommy, when some men go off to war, they leave as men and return as children." My Uncle Ralph had returned from war as a child with a Purple Heart that he had earned as a man. Uncle Ralph came home from his stay at the VA hospital several months later. Aunt Ray was waiting for him with unconditional love.

These were the first experiences I ever had with a war veteran. They were unique experiences, and yet somewhat insightful for what I would later learn.

## The Purpose.

Almost half a century after those first overheard conversations at home, I was honored to spend a year of my life crisscrossing the United States visiting with and photographing 48 of the living Medal of Honor Recipients.

These men and their legacy are one of our country's best kept secrets. They are some of the finest role models and heroes our country has to offer — living examples of the best of our human character.

I found that most of the existing photographs of these individuals were from their service days or posed, formal photographs with The Medal draped around their necks. But I didn't want to look at these men in a mindset of formality or military citation and battlefield actions. I wanted to discover what was beyond the surface, beyond the actions that took place some 30 to 50 years before. I wanted to see them as they really are; as they view themselves; as ordinary men.

## The Experience.

It was a privilege to meet with these men in their homes; to laugh and sometimes cry with them; to look into their eyes and witness their fortitude, compassion and love of patriotism and freedom.

These are ordinary men living ordinary lives. Like you and me, they love their families, attend their churches, and give of themselves to their communities. They have their triumphs and challenges. And, as I visited with them, one-on-one, I found myself telling them that I was trying to capture the spirit of the group, the thread that linked them all together, the spirit that made heroes out of "ordinary" men.

As my journey progressed, I became more and more fascinated with the courage these men live with daily. It's as if they live two lives: their everyday lives, and the lives of Medal of Honor Recipients.

Although people are awed by their battlefield actions, these men were the first to tell me that they really didn't do anything that hundreds of thousands of other men and women hadn't done before them and after them in battle. They were simply doing their duty to the best of their abilities.

What makes these select few "different" is that they have the honor (or burden, as some have described it) of wearing The Medal of Honor for the rest of their lives. They see themselves as simply "caretakers" of The Medal for those who fought and died and received no recognition; for those who, but for an act of God, would be wearing The Medal today. They share the responsibility of The Medal with all who have fought — and all who have died — for our country. And they would like to share The Medal with everyone else, using their personal achievements to help us find the potential that lies within each and every one of us.

## Making It Personal.

When we learn about these men, we are overwhelmed by their patriotism and battlefield heroics, and we must ask the inner-personal questions: "Could I have done that? Would I have had the courage to have conducted myself in the same way?" Again, in their words, they were simply doing their duty. Yet, we must wonder about the extraordinary spirit that allowed them to persevere through nearly impossible circumstances. Does our interest in them help fill a void in our own lives? Do their experiences bring meaning to us?

Part of the spirit of these remarkable individuals is that every day of their lives they honor the value of freedom for every person in our country and in the world. As such, they hold high expectations for us all. They want each of us to be the best parent, husband, wife, sister, brother, son, daughter and friend we can be. They urge us to live, laugh, cry, love, forgive, respect and honor one another. And, most importantly, they tell us to hold fast to our God, seek our God for guidance and strength. This is their vision of our duty, as ordinary men and women.

## The Spirit.

I believe that I have found the true spirit of this elite group. Through the experience of visiting with and photographing these men, I have been awakened to the "wonderfulness of ordinary."

Too often we become overwhelmed with daily life — keeping up, keeping pace, looking in all the wrong places for heroes and role models. We lose sight of the strength and courage it takes just to be ordinary. Yet the real beauty of life lies in just doing our daily duty to all, for all, through small acts of kindness and love. These are the actions that build strong families, strong communities and strong spiritual values. These are the acts that build patriotism and are the foundation of the freedoms we cherish.

## The Message.

The Medal of Honor Recipients featured in this book invite you to seek the strength and heroism in your own spirit — the hero that you are. They encourage you to embrace your "ordinary" life, realize your own "wonderfulness of ordinary," and discover that you, too, can have the courage to be fearless while loving your God, yourself and your fellow man. You have the inner spirit to do your duty, every day.

With all my heart, I thank these men for allowing me to come into their lives, for giving me this gift, and for trusting me to share it with you.

Please use these photographs to take your own journey — to meet these heroes, and to see how truly beautiful "ordinary" can be.

# The Congressional Medal of Honor Citations

*There are three different types of Medals of Honor today: the original simple star shape established in 1861, which the Navy, Marine Corps and Coast Guard have retained (left); a wreath version designed in 1904 for the Army (right); and an altered wreath version for the Air Force, adopted in 1965 (center).*

## Barfoot, Van T.

**Rank and organization:**
Second Lieutenant, U.S. Army,
157th Infantry, 45th Infantry Division.
**Place and date:**
Near Carano, Italy, 23 May 1944.
**Entered service at:**
Carthage, Miss.
**Birth:**
Edinburg, Miss.
**G.O. No.:**
79, 4 October 1944.

**Citation:**
For conspicuous gallantry and intrepidity at the risk of life above and beyond the call of duty on 23 May 1944, near Carano, Italy. With his platoon heavily engaged during an assault against forces well entrenched on commanding ground, 2d Lt. Barfoot (then Tech. Sgt.) moved off alone upon the enemy left flank. He crawled to the proximity of 1 machine-gun nest and made a direct hit on it with a handgrenade, killing 2 and wounding 3 Germans. He continued along the German defense line to another machine-gun emplacement, and with his tommygun killed 2 and captured 3 soldiers. Members of another enemy machine-gun crew then abandoned their position and gave themselves up to Sgt. Barfoot. Leaving the prisoners for his support squad to pick up, he proceeded to mop up positions in the immediate area, capturing more prisoners and bringing his total count to 17. Later that day, after he had reorganized his men and consolidated the newly captured ground, the enemy launched a fierce armored counterattack directly at his platoon positions. Securing a bazooka, Sgt. Barfoot took up an exposed position directly in front of 3 advancing Mark VI tanks. From a distance of 75 yards his first shot destroyed the track of the leading tank, effectively disabling it, while the other 2 changed direction toward the flank. As the crew of the disabled tank dismounted, Sgt. Barfoot killed 3 of them with his tommygun. He continued onward into enemy terrain and destroyed a recently abandoned German fieldpiece with a demolition charge placed in the breech. While returning to his platoon position, Sgt. Barfoot, though greatly fatigued by his herculean efforts, assisted 2 of his seriously wounded men 1,700 yards to a position of safety. Sgt. Barfoot's extraordinary heroism, demonstration of magnificent valor, and aggressive determination in the face of pointblank fire are a perpetual inspiration to his fellow soldiers.

## Barnum, Harvey C., Jr.

**Rank and organization:**
Captain (then Lt.), U.S. Marine Corps,
Company H, 2d Battalion, 9th Marines,
3d Marine Division (Rein).
**Place and date:**
Ky Phu in Quang Tin Province,
Republic of Vietnam, 18 December 1965.
**Entered service at:**
Cheshire, Conn.
**Born:**
21 July 1940, Cheshire, Conn.

**Citation:**
For conspicuous gallantry and intrepidity at the risk of his life above and beyond the call of duty. When the company was suddenly pinned down by a hail of extremely accurate enemy fire and was quickly separated from the remainder of the battalion by over 500 meters of open and fire-swept ground, and casualties mounted rapidly, Lt. Barnum quickly made a hazardous reconnaissance of the area, seeking targets for his artillery. Finding the rifle company commander mortally wounded and the radio operator killed, he, with complete disregard for his safety, gave aid to the dying commander, then removed the radio from the dead operator and strapped it to himself. He immediately assumed command of the rifle company, and moving at once into the midst of the heavy fire, rallying and giving encouragement to all units, reorganized them to replace the loss of key personnel and led their attack on enemy positions from which deadly fire continued to come. His sound and swift decisions and his obvious calm served to stabilize the badly decimated units and his gallant example as he stood exposed repeatedly to point out targets served as an inspiration to all. Provided with 2 armed helicopters, he moved fearlessly through enemy fire to control the air attack against the firmly entrenched enemy

while skillfully directing 1 platoon in a successful counterattack on the key enemy positions. Having thus cleared a small area, he requested and directed the landing of 2 transport helicopters for the evacuation of the dead and wounded. He then assisted in the mopping up and final seizure of the battalion's objective. His gallant initiative and heroic conduct reflected great credit upon himself and were in keeping with the highest traditions of the Marine Corps and the U.S. Naval Service.

## Biddle, Melvin E.

**Rank and organization:**
Private First Class, U.S. Army, Company B, 517th Parachute Infantry Regiment.
**Place and date:**
Near Soy, Belgium,
23-24 December 1944.
**Entered service at:**
Anderson, Ind.
**Birth:**
Daleville, Ind.
**G.O. No.:**
95, 30 October 1945.

**Citation:**
He displayed conspicuous gallantry and intrepidity in action against the enemy near Soy, Belgium, on 23 and 24 December 1944. Serving as lead scout during an attack to relieve the enemy-encircled town of Hotton, he aggressively penetrated a densely wooded area, advanced 400 yards until he came within range of intense enemy rifle fire, and

within 20 yards of enemy positions killed 3 snipers with unerring marksmanship. Courageously continuing his advance an additional 200 yards, he discovered a hostile machine-gun position and dispatched its 2 occupants. He then located the approximate position of a well-concealed enemy machine-gun nest, and crawling forward threw handgrenades which killed two Germans and fatally wounded a third. After signaling his company to advance, he entered a determined line of enemy defense, coolly and deliberately shifted his position, and shot 3 more enemy soldiers. Undaunted by enemy fire, he crawled within 20 yards of a machine-gun nest, tossed his last handgrenade into the position, and after the explosion charged the emplacement firing his rifle. When night fell, he scouted enemy positions alone for several hours and returned with valuable information which enabled our attacking infantry and armor to knock out 2 enemy tanks. At daybreak he again led the advance and, when flanking elements were pinned down by enemy fire, without hesitation made his way toward a hostile machine-gun position and from a distance of 50 yards killed the crew and 2 supporting riflemen. The remainder of the enemy, finding themselves without automatic weapon support, fled panic stricken. Pfc. Biddle's intrepid courage and superb daring during his 20-hour action enabled his battalion to break the enemy grasp on Hotton with a minimum of casualties.

## Burt, James M.

**Rank and organization:**
Captain, U.S. Army, Company B,
66th Armored Regiment,
2d Armored Division.
**Place and date:**
Near Wurselen, Germany,
13 October 1944.
**Entered service at:**
Lee, Mass.
**Birth:**
Hinsdale, Mass.
**G.O. No.:**
95, 30 October 1945.

**Citation:**
Capt. James M. Burt was in command of Company B, 66th Armored Regiment on the western outskirts of Wurselen, Germany, on 13 October 1944, when his organization participated in a coordinated infantry-tank attack destined to isolate the large German garrison which was tenaciously defending the city of Aachen. In the first day's action, when infantrymen ran into murderous small-arms and mortar fire, Capt. Burt dismounted from his tank about 200 yards to the rear and moved forward on foot beyond the infantry positions, where, as the enemy concentrated a tremendous volume of fire upon him, he calmly motioned his tanks into good firing positions. As our attack gained momentum, he climbed aboard his tank and directed the action from the rear deck, exposed to hostile volleys which finally wounded him painfully in the face

and neck. He maintained his dangerous post despite pointblank self-propelled gunfire until friendly artillery knocked out these enemy weapons, and then proceeded to the advanced infantry scouts' positions to deploy his tanks for the defense of the gains which had been made. The next day, when the enemy counterattacked, he left cover and went 75 yards through heavy fire to assist the infantry battalion commander who was seriously wounded. For the next 8 days, through rainy, miserable weather and under constant, heavy shelling, Capt. Burt held the combined forces together, dominating and controlling the critical situation through the sheer force of his heroic example. To direct artillery fire, on 15 October, he took his tank 300 yards into the enemy lines, where he dismounted and remained for 1 hour giving accurate data to friendly gunners. Twice more that day he went into enemy territory under deadly fire on reconnaissance. In succeeding days he never faltered in his determination to defeat the strong German forces opposing him. Twice the tank in which he was riding was knocked out by enemy action, and each time he climbed aboard another vehicle and continued the fight. He took great risks to rescue wounded comrades and inflicted prodigious destruction on enemy personnel and materiel even though suffering from the wounds he received in the battle's opening phase. Capt. Burt's intrepidity

and disregard of personal safety were so complete that his own men and the infantry who attached themselves to him were inspired to overcome the wretched and extremely hazardous conditions which accompanied one of the most bitter local actions of the war. The victory achieved closed the Aachen gap.

## Bush, Robert Eugene

**Rank and organization:**
Hospital Apprentice First Class, U.S. Naval Reserve, serving as Medical Corpsman with a rifle company, 2d Battalion, 5th Marines, 1st Marine Division.
**Place and date:**
Okinawa Jima, Ryukyu Islands, 2 May 1945.
**Entered service at:**
Washington.
**Born:**
4 October 1926, Tacoma, Wash.

**Citation:**
For conspicuous gallantry and intrepidity at the risk of his life above and beyond the call of duty while serving as Medical Corpsman with a rifle company, in action against enemy Japanese forces on Okinawa Jima, Ryukyu Islands, 2 May 1945. Fearlessly braving the fury of artillery, mortar, and machine-gun fire from strongly entrenched hostile positions, Bush constantly and unhesitatingly moved from 1 casualty to another to attend the wounded falling under the enemy's murderous barrages.

As the attack passed over a ridge top, Bush was advancing to administer blood plasma to a marine officer lying wounded on the skyline when the Japanese launched a savage counterattack. In this perilously exposed position, he resolutely maintained the flow of life-giving plasma. With the bottle held high in 1 hand, Bush drew his pistol with the other and fired into the enemy ranks until his ammunition was expended. Quickly seizing a discarded carbine, he trained his fire on the Japanese charging pointblank over the hill, accounting for 6 of the enemy despite his own serious wounds and the loss of 1 eye suffered during his desperate battle in defense of the helpless man. With the hostile force finally routed, he calmly disregarded his own critical condition to complete his mission, valiantly refusing medical treatment for himself until his officer patient had been evacuated, and collapsing only after attempting to walk to the battle aid station. His daring initiative, great personal valor, and heroic spirit of self-sacrifice in service of others reflect great credit upon Bush and enhance the finest traditions of the U.S. Naval Service.

## Cavaiani, Jon R.

**Rank and organization:**
Staff Sergeant, U.S. Army, Vietnam Training Advisory Group, Republic of Vietnam.

**Place and date:**
Republic of Vietnam, 4 and 5 June 1971.
**Entered service at:**
Fresno, Calif.
**Born:**
2 August 1943, Royston, England.

**Citation:**
S/Sgt. Cavaiani distinguished himself by conspicuous gallantry and intrepidity at the risk of life above and beyond the call of duty in action in the Republic of Vietnam on 4 and 5 June 1971 while serving as a platoon leader to a security platoon providing security for an isolated radio relay site located within enemy-held territory. On the morning of 4 June 1971, the entire camp came under an intense barrage of enemy small arms, automatic weapons, rocket-propelled grenade and mortar fire from a superior size enemy force. S/Sgt. Cavaiani acted with complete disregard for his personal safety as he repeatedly exposed himself to heavy enemy fire in order to move about the camp's perimeter directing the platoon's fire and rallying the platoon in a desperate fight for survival. S/Sgt. Cavaiani also returned heavy suppressive fire upon the assaulting enemy force during this period with a variety of weapons. When the entire platoon was to be evacuated, S/Sgt. Cavaiani unhesitatingly volunteered to remain on the ground and direct the helicopters into the landing zone. S/Sgt. Cavaiani was able to direct the first 3 helicopters in evacuating a major portion of the platoon. Due to intense increase in enemy fire, S/Sgt. Cavaiani was forced to remain at the camp overnight where he calmly directed the remaining platoon members in strengthening their defenses. On the morning of 5 June, a heavy ground fog restricted visibility. The superior size enemy force launched a major ground attack in an attempt to completely annihilate the remaining small force. The enemy force advanced in 2 ranks, first firing a heavy volume of small arms automatic weapons and rocket-propelled grenade fire while the second rank continuously threw a steady barrage of handgrenades at the beleaguered force. S/Sgt. Cavaiani returned a heavy barrage of small arms and handgrenade fire on the assaulting enemy force but was unable to slow them down. He ordered the remaining platoon members to attempt to escape while he provided them with cover fire. With 1 last courageous exertion, S/Sgt. Cavaiani recovered a machine-gun, stood up, completely exposing himself to the heavy enemy fire directed at him, and began firing the machine-gun in a sweeping motion along the 2 ranks of advancing enemy soldiers. Through S/Sgt. Cavaiani's valiant efforts with complete disregard for his safety, the majority of the remaining platoon members were able to escape. While inflicting severe losses on the advancing enemy force, S/Sgt. Cavaiani was wounded numerous times. S/Sgt. Cavaiani's conspicuous gallantry, extraordinary heroism and intrepidity at the risk of his life, above and beyond the call of duty, were in keeping with the highest traditions of the military service and reflect great credit upon himself and the U.S. Army.

## Childers, Ernest

**Rank and organization:**
Second Lieutenant, U.S. Army, 45th Infantry Division.
**Place and date:**
At Oliveto, Italy, 22 September 1943.
**Entered service at:**
Tulsa, Okla.
**Birth:**
Broken Arrow, Okla.
**G.O. No.:**
30, 8 April 1944.

**Citation:**
For conspicuous gallantry and intrepidity at risk of life above and beyond the call of duty in action on 22 September 1943, at Oliveto, Italy. Although 2d Lt. Childers previously had just suffered a fractured instep he, with 8 enlisted men, advanced up a hill toward enemy machine-gun nests. The group advanced to a rock wall overlooking a cornfield and 2d Lt. Childers ordered a base of fire laid across the field so that he could advance. When he was fired upon by 2 enemy

snipers from a nearby house he killed both of them. He moved behind the machine-gun nests and killed all occupants of the nearer one. He continued toward the second one and threw rocks into it. When the 2 occupants of the nest raised up, he shot 1. The other was killed by 1 of the 8 enlisted men. 2d Lt. Childers continued his advance toward a house farther up the hill, and single-handed, captured an enemy mortar observer. The exceptional leadership, initiative, calmness under fire, and conspicuous gallantry displayed by 2d Lt. Childers were an inspiration to his men.

## Crews, John R.

**Rank and organization:**
Staff Sergeant, U.S. Army, Company F, 253d Infantry, 63d Infantry Division.
**Place and date:**
Near Lobenbacherhof, Germany, 8 April 1945.
**Entered service at:**
Bowlegs, Okla.
**Birth:**
Golden, Okla.

**Citation:**
He displayed conspicuous gallantry and intrepidity at the risk of his life above and beyond the call of duty on 8 April 1945 near Lobenbacherhof, Germany.

As his company was advancing toward the village under heavy fire, an enemy machine-gun and automatic rifle with rifle support opened upon it from a hill on the right flank. Seeing that his platoon leader had been wounded by their fire, S/Sgt. Crews, acting on his own initiative, rushed the strongpoint with 2 men of his platoon. Despite the fact that 1 of these men was killed and the other was badly wounded, he continued his advance up the hill in the face of terrific enemy fire. Storming the well-dug-in position single-handedly, he killed 2 of the crew of the machine-gun at pointblank range with his M1 rifle and wrestled the gun from the hands of the German whom he had already wounded. He then with his rifle charged the strongly emplaced automatic rifle. Although badly wounded in the thigh by crossfire from the remaining enemy, he kept on and silenced the entire position with his accurate and deadly rifle fire. His actions so unnerved the remaining enemy soldiers that 7 of them surrendered and the others fled. His heroism caused the enemy to concentrate on him and permitted the company to move forward into the village.

## Currey, Francis S.

**Rank and organization:**
Sergeant, U.S. Army, Company K, 120th Infantry, 30th Infantry Division.

**Place and date:**
Malmedy, Belgium, 21 December 1944.
**Entered service at:**
Hurleyville, N.Y.
**Birth:**
Loch Sheldrake, N.Y.
**G.O. No.:**
69, 17 August 1945.

**Citation:**
He was an automatic rifleman with the 3d Platoon defending a strong point near Malmedy, Belgium, on 21 December 1944, when the enemy launched a powerful attack. Overrunning tank destroyers and antitank guns located near the strong point, German tanks advanced to the 3d Platoon's position, and, after prolonged fighting, forced the withdrawal of this group to a nearby factory. Sgt. Currey found a bazooka in the building and crossed the street to secure rockets meanwhile enduring intense fire from enemy tanks and hostile infantrymen who had taken up a position at a house a short distance away. In the face of small-arms, machine-gun, and artillery fire, he, with a companion, knocked out a tank with 1 shot. Moving to another position, he observed 3 Germans in the doorway of an enemy-held house. He killed or wounded all 3 with his automatic rifle. He emerged from cover and advanced alone to within 50 yards of the house, intent on

wrecking it with rockets. Covered by friendly fire, he stood erect, and fired a shot which knocked down half of 1 wall. While in this forward position, he observed 5 Americans who had been pinned down for hours by fire from the house and 3 tanks. Realizing that they could not escape until the enemy tank and infantry guns had been silenced, Sgt. Currey crossed the street to a vehicle, where he procured an armful of antitank grenades. These he launched while under heavy enemy fire, driving the tankmen from the vehicles into the house. He then climbed onto a halftrack in full view of the Germans and fired a machine-gun at the house. Once again changing his position, he manned another machine-gun whose crew had been killed; under his covering fire the 5 soldiers were able to retire to safety. Deprived of tanks and with heavy infantry casualties, the enemy was forced to withdraw. Through his extensive knowledge of weapons and by his heroic and repeated braving of murderous enemy fire, Sgt. Currey was greatly responsible for inflicting heavy losses in men and material on the enemy, for rescuing 5 comrades, 2 of whom were wounded, and for stemming an attack which threatened to flank his battalion's position.

# Davis, Raymond G.

**Rank and organization:**
Lieutenant Colonel, U.S. Marine Corps, commanding officer, 1st Battalion, 7th Marines, 1st Marine Division (Rein).
**Place and date:**
Vicinity Hagaru-ri, Korea,
1 through 4 December 1950.
**Entered service at:**
Atlanta, Ga.
**Born:**
13 January 1915, Fitzgerald, Ga.

**Citation:**
For conspicuous gallantry and intrepidity at the risk of his life above and beyond the call of duty as commanding officer of the 1st Battalion, in action against enemy aggressor forces. Although keenly aware that the operation involved breaking through a surrounding enemy and advancing 8 miles along primitive icy trails in the bitter cold with every passage disputed by a savage and determined foe, Lt. Col. Davis boldly lead his battalion into the attack in a daring attempt to relieve a beleaguered rifle company and to seize, hold, and defend a vital mountain pass controlling the only route available for 2 marine regiments in danger of being cut off by numerically superior hostile forces during their redeployment to the port of Hungnam. When the battalion immediately encountered strong opposition from entrenched enemy

forces commanding high ground in the path of the advance, he promptly spearheaded his unit in a fierce attack up the steep, ice-covered slopes in the face of withering fire and, personally leading the assault groups in a hand-to-hand encounter, drove the hostile troops from their positions, rested his men, and reconnoitered the area under enemy fire to determine the best route for continuing the mission. Always in the thick of the fighting Lt. Col. Davis led his battalion over 3 successive ridges in the deep snow in continuous attacks against the enemy and, constantly inspiring and encouraging his men throughout the night, brought his unit to a point within 1,500 yards of the surrounded rifle company by daybreak. Although knocked to the ground when a shell fragment struck his helmet and 2 bullets pierced his clothing, he arose and fought his way forward at the head of his men until he reached the isolated marines. On the following morning, he bravely led his battalion in securing the vital mountain pass from a strongly entrenched and numerically superior hostile force, carrying all his wounded with him, including 22 litter cases and numerous ambulatory patients. Despite repeated savage and heavy assaults by the enemy, he stubbornly held the vital terrain until the 2 regiments of the division had deployed through the pass and, on the morning of 4 December, led his battalion into Hagaru-ri intact. By his superb leadership, outstanding courage, and brilliant tactical ability, Lt. Col. Davis was directly instrumental in saving the beleaguered rifle company from complete annihilation and enabled the 2 marine regiments to escape possible destruction. His valiant devotion to duty and unyielding fighting spirit in the face of almost insurmountable odds enhance and sustain the highest traditions of the U.S. Naval Service.

## Davis, Sammy L.

**Rank and organization:**
Sergeant, U.S. Army, Battery C,
2d Battalion, 4th Artillery,
9th Infantry Division.
**Place and date:**
West of Cai Lay, Republic of Vietnam,
18 November 1967.
**Entered service at:**
Indianapolis, Ind.
**Born:**
1 November 1946, Dayton, Ohio.

**Citation:**
For conspicuous gallantry and intrepidity in action at the risk of his life and beyond the call of duty. Sgt. Davis (then Pfc.) distinguished himself during the early morning hours while serving as a cannoneer with Battery C, at a remote fire support base. At approximately 0200 hours, the fire support base was under heavy enemy mortar attack. Simultaneously, an estimated reinforced Viet Cong battalion launched a fierce ground assault upon the fire support base. The attacking enemy drove to within 25 meters of the friendly positions. Only a river separated the Viet Cong from the fire support base. Detecting a nearby enemy position, Sgt. Davis seized a machine-gun and provided covering fire for his guncrew, as they attempted to bring direct artillery fire on the enemy. Despite his efforts, an enemy recoilless rifle round scored a direct hit upon the artillery piece. The resultant blast hurled the guncrew from their weapon and blew Sgt. Davis into a foxhole. He struggled to his feet and returned to the howitzer, which was burning furiously. Ignoring repeated warnings to seek cover, Sgt. Davis rammed a shell into the gun. Disregarding a withering hail of enemy fire directed against his position, he aimed and fired the howitzer which rolled backward, knocking Sgt. Davis violently to the ground. Undaunted, he returned to the weapon to fire again when an enemy mortar round exploded within 20 meters of his position, injuring him painfully. Nevertheless, Sgt. Davis loaded the artillery piece, aimed and fired. Again he was knocked down by the recoil. In complete disregard for his safety, Sgt. Davis loaded and fired 3 more shells into the enemy. Disregarding his extensive injuries and his inability to swim, Sgt. Davis picked up an air mattress and struck out across the deep river to rescue 3 wounded comrades on the far side. Upon reaching the 3 wounded men, he stood upright and fired into the dense vegetation to prevent the Viet Cong from advancing. While the most seriously wounded soldier was helped across the river, Sgt. Davis protected the 2 remaining casualties until he could pull them across the river to the fire support base. Though suffering from painful wounds, he refused medical attention, joining another howitzer crew which fired at the large Viet Cong force until it broke contact and fled. Sgt. Davis' extraordinary heroism, at the risk of his life, are in keeping with the highest traditions of the military service and reflect great credit upon himself and the U.S. Army.

## Doss, Desmond T.

**Rank and organization:**
Private First Class, U.S. Army,
Medical Detachment, 307th Infantry,
77th Infantry Division.
**Place and date:**
Near Urasoe-Mura, Okinawa, Ryukyu
Islands, 29 April-21 May 1945.
**Entered service at:**
Lynchburg, Va.
**Birth:**
Lynchburg, Va.
**G.O. No.:**
97, 1 November 1945.

*Citation:*

He was a company aid man when the 1st Battalion assaulted a jagged escarpment 400 feet high. As our troops gained the summit, a heavy concentration of artillery, mortar and machine-gun fire crashed into them, inflicting approximately 75 casualties and driving the others back. Pfc. Doss refused to seek cover and remained in the fire-swept area with the many stricken, carrying them 1 by 1 to the edge of the escarpment and there lowering them on a rope-supported litter down the face of a cliff to friendly hands. On 2 May, he exposed himself to heavy rifle and mortar fire in rescuing a wounded man 200 yards forward of the lines on the same escarpment; and 2 days later he treated 4 men who had been cut down while assaulting a strongly defended cave, advancing through a shower of grenades to within 8 yards of enemy forces in a cave's mouth, where he dressed his comrades' wounds before making 4 separate trips under fire to evacuate them to safety. On 5 May, he unhesitatingly braved enemy shelling and small-arms fire to assist an artillery officer. He applied bandages, moved his patient to a spot that offered protection from small-arms fire and, while artillery and mortar shells fell close by, painstakingly administered plasma. Later that day, when an American was severely wounded by fire from a cave, Pfc. Doss crawled to him where he had fallen 25 feet from the enemy position, rendered aid, and carried him 100 yards to safety while continually exposed to enemy fire. On 21 May, in a night attack on high ground near Shuri, he remained in exposed territory while the rest of his company took cover, fearlessly risking the chance that he would be mistaken for an infiltrating Japanese and giving aid to the injured until he was himself seriously wounded in the legs by the explosion of a grenade. Rather than call another aid man from cover, he cared for his own injuries and waited 5 hours before litter bearers reached him and started carrying him to cover. The trio was caught in an enemy tank attack and Pfc. Doss, seeing a more critically wounded man nearby, crawled off the litter and directed the bearers to give their first attention to the other man. Awaiting the litter bearers' return, he was again struck, this time suffering a compound fracture of 1 arm. With magnificent fortitude he bound a rifle stock to his shattered arm as a splint and then crawled 300 yards over rough terrain to the aid station. Through his outstanding bravery and unflinching determination in the face of desperately dangerous conditions Pfc. Doss saved the lives of many soldiers. His name became a symbol throughout the 77th Infantry Division for outstanding gallantry far above and beyond the call of duty.

*Dunham, Russell E.*

**Rank and organization:**
Technical Sergeant, U.S. Army, Company I, 30th Infantry, 3d Infantry Division.

**Place and date:**
Near Kayserberg, France, 8 January 1945.
**Entered service at:**
Brighton Ill.
**Born:**
23 February 1920, East Carondelet, Ill.
**G.O. No.:**
37, 11 May 1945.

*Citation:*

For conspicuous gallantry and intrepidity at risk of life above and beyond the call of duty. At about 1430 hours on 8 January 1945, during an attack on Hill 616, near Kayserberg, France, T/Sgt. Dunham single-handedly assaulted 3 enemy machine-guns. Wearing a white robe made of a mattress cover, carrying 12 carbine magazines and with a dozen handgrenades snagged in his belt, suspenders, and buttonholes, T/Sgt. Dunham advanced in the attack up a snow-covered hill under fire from 2 machine-guns and supporting riflemen. His platoon 35 yards behind him, T/Sgt. Dunham crawled 75 yards under heavy direct fire toward the timbered emplacement shielding the left machine-gun. As he jumped to his feet 10 yards from the gun and charged forward, machine-gun fire tore through his camouflage robe and a rifle bullet seared a 10-inch gash across his back sending him spinning 15 yards down hill into the snow. When the indomitable sergeant sprang to his feet to renew his 1-man assault, a German egg grenade landed beside him. He kicked it aside, and as it exploded 5 yards away, shot and killed the German machine-gunner and assistant gunner. His carbine empty, he jumped into the emplacement and hauled out the third member of the gun crew by the collar. Although his back wound was causing him excruciating pain and blood was seeping through his white coat, T/Sgt. Dunham proceeded 50 yards through a storm of automatic and rifle fire to attack the second machine-gun. Twenty-five yards from the emplacement he hurled 2 grenades, destroying the gun and its crew; then fired down into the supporting foxholes with his carbine, dispatching and dispersing the enemy riflemen. Although his coat was so thoroughly blood-soaked that he was a conspicuous target against the white landscape, T/Sgt. Dunham again advanced ahead of his platoon in an assault on enemy positions farther up the hill. Coming under machine-gun fire from 65 yards to his front, while rifle grenades exploded 10 yards from his position, he hit the ground and crawled forward. At 15 yards range, he jumped to his feet, staggered a few paces toward the timbered machine-gun emplacement and killed the crew with handgrenades. An enemy rifleman fired at pointblank range, but missed him. After killing the riflemen, T/Sgt. Dunham drove others from their foxholes with grenades and carbine fire. Killing 9 Germans — wounding 7 and capturing 2 — firing about 175 rounds of carbine ammunition,

and expending 11 grenades, T/Sgt. Dunham, despite a painful wound, spearheaded a spectacular and successful diversionary attack.

## Ehlers, Walter D.

**Rank and organization:**
Staff Sergeant, U.S. Army, 18th Infantry, 1st Infantry Division.
**Place and date:**
Near Goville, France, 9-10 June 1944.
**Entered service at:**
Manhattan, Kans.
**Birth:**
Junction City, Kans.
**G.O. No.:**
91, 19 December 1944.

**Citation:**
For conspicuous gallantry and intrepidity at the risk of his life above and beyond the call of duty on 9-10 June 1944, near Goville, France. S/Sgt. Ehlers, always acting as the spearhead of the attack, repeatedly led his men against heavily defended enemy strong points exposing himself to deadly hostile fire whenever the situation required heroic and courageous leadership. Without waiting for an order, S/Sgt. Ehlers, far ahead of his men, led his squad against a strongly defended enemy strong point, personally killing 4 of an enemy patrol who attacked him en route. Then crawling forward under withering machine-gun fire, he pounced upon the guncrew and put it out of action. Turning his attention

to 2 mortars protected by the crossfire of 2 machine-guns, S/Sgt. Ehlers led his men through this hail of bullets to kill or put to flight the enemy of the mortar section, killing 3 men himself. After mopping up the mortar positions, he again advanced on a machine-gun, his progress effectively covered by his squad. When he was almost on top of the gun he leaped to his feet and, although greatly outnumbered, he knocked out the position single-handed. The next day, having advanced deep into enemy territory, the platoon of which S/Sgt. Ehlers was a member, finding itself in an untenable position as the enemy brought increased mortar, machine-gun, and small-arms fire to bear on it, was ordered to withdraw. S/Sgt. Ehlers, after his squad had covered the withdrawal of the remainder of the platoon, stood up and by continuous fire at the semicircle of enemy placements, diverted the bulk of the heavy hostile fire on himself, thus permitting the members of his own squad to withdraw. At this point, though wounded himself, he carried his wounded automatic rifleman to safety and then returned fearlessly over the shell-swept field to retrieve the automatic rifle which he was unable to carry previously. After having his wound treated, he refused to be evacuated, and returned to lead his squad. The intrepid leadership, indomitable courage, and fearless aggressiveness displayed by S/Sgt. Ehlers in the face of overwhelming enemy forces serve as an inspiration to others.

## Finn, John William

**Rank and organization:**
Lieutenant, U.S. Navy.
**Place and date:**
Naval Air Station, Kaneohe Bay,
Territory of Hawaii, 7 December 1941.
**Entered service at:**
California.
**Born:**
23 July 1909, Los Angeles, Calif.

**Citation:**
For extraordinary heroism distinguished
service, and devotion above and beyond
the call of duty. During the first attack by
Japanese airplanes on the Naval Air
Station, Kaneohe Bay, on 7 December
1941, Lt. Finn promptly secured and
manned a .50-caliber machine-gun
mounted on an instruction stand in a
completely exposed section of the
parking ramp, which was under heavy
enemy machine-gun strafing fire.
Although painfully wounded many times,
he continued to man this gun and to
return the enemy's fire vigorously and
with telling effect throughout the enemy
strafing and bombing attacks and with
complete disregard for his own personal
safety. It was only by specific orders that
he was persuaded to leave his post to
seek medical attention. Following
first-aid treatment, although obviously
suffering much pain and moving
with great difficulty, he returned to
the squadron area and actively
supervised the rearming of returning
planes. His extraordinary heroism
and conduct in this action were in
keeping with the highest traditions of
the U.S. Naval Service.

## Fitzmaurice, Michael John

**Rank and organization:**
Specialist Fourth Class, U.S. Army,
Troop D, 2d Squadron, 17th Cavalry,
101st Airborne Division.
**Place and date:**
Khesanh, Republic of Vietnam,
23 March 1971.
**Entered service at:**
Sioux Falls, S. Dak.
**Born:**
9 March 1950, Jamestown, N. Dak.

**Citation:**
For conspicuous gallantry and intrepidity
in action at the risk of his life
above and beyond the call of duty.
Sp4c. Fitzmaurice, 3d Platoon, Troop D,
distinguished himself at Khesanh.
Sp4c Fitzmaurice and 3 fellow soldiers
were occupying a bunker when a
company of North Vietnamese sappers
infiltrated the area. At the onset of the
attack Sp4c. Fitzmaurice observed
3 explosive charges which had been
thrown into the bunker by the enemy.
Realizing the imminent danger to his
comrades, and with complete disregard
for his personal safety, he hurled 2 of
the charges out of the bunker. He then
threw his flak vest and himself over the
remaining charge. By this courageous act
he absorbed the blast and shielded his
fellow-soldiers. Although suffering from
serious multiple wounds and partial loss
of sight, he charged out of the bunker,
and engaged the enemy until his rifle
was damaged by the blast of an enemy
handgrenade. While in search of another
weapon, Sp4c. Fitzmaurice encountered
and overcame an enemy sapper in
hand-to-hand combat. Having obtained
another weapon, he returned to his
original fighting position and inflicted
additional casualties on the attacking
enemy. Although seriously wounded,
Sp4c. Fitzmaurice refused to be
medically evacuated, preferring to
remain at his post. Sp4c. Fitzmaurice's
extraordinary heroism in action at the
risk of his life contributed significantly
to the successful defense of the position
and resulted in saving the lives of a
number of his fellow soldiers. These acts
of heroism go above and beyond the call
of duty, are in keeping with the highest
traditions of the military service, and
reflect great credit on Sp4c. Fitzmaurice
and the U.S. Army.

## Fritz, Harold A.

**Rank and organization:**
Captain, U.S. Army, Troop A,
1st Squadron, 11th Armored
Cavalry Regiment.
**Place and date:**
Binh Long Province, Republic of
Vietnam, 11 January 1969.
**Entered service at:**
Milwaukee, Wis.
**Born:**
21 February 1944, Chicago, Ill.

**Citation:**
For conspicuous gallantry and intrepidity
in action at the risk of his life above
and beyond the call of duty.
Capt. (then 1st Lt.) Fritz, Armor, U.S.
Army, distinguished himself while
serving as a platoon leader with Troop A,
near Quan Loi. Capt. Fritz was leading
his 7-vehicle armored column along
Highway 13 to meet and escort a truck
convoy when the column suddenly came
under intense crossfire from a reinforced
enemy company deployed in ambush
positions. In the initial attack, Capt. Fritz'
vehicle was hit and he was seriously
wounded. Realizing that his platoon was
completely surrounded, vastly
outnumbered, and in danger of being
overrun, Capt. Fritz leaped to the top of
his burning vehicle and directed the
positioning of his remaining vehicles and
men. With complete disregard for his
wounds and safety, he ran from vehicle
to vehicle in complete view of the enemy
gunners in order to reposition his men,
to improve the defense, to assist the
wounded, to distribute ammunition, to
direct fire, and to provide encouragement
to his men. When a strong enemy force
assaulted the position and attempted to
overrun the platoon, Capt. Fritz manned
a machine-gun and through his
exemplary action inspired his men to
deliver intense and deadly fire which
broke the assault and routed the
attackers. Moments later a second enemy
force advanced to within 2 meters of the
position and threatened to overwhelm
the defenders. Capt. Fritz, armed only
with a pistol and bayonet, led a small
group of his men in a fierce and daring
charge which routed the attackers and
inflicted heavy casualties. When a relief
force arrived, Capt. Fritz saw that it was
not deploying effectively against the
enemy positions, and he moved through
the heavy enemy fire to direct its
deployment against the hostile positions.
This deployment forced the enemy to
abandon the ambush site and withdraw.
Despite his wounds, Capt. Fritz returned
to his position, assisted his men, and
refused medical attention until all of his
wounded comrades had been treated and
evacuated. The extraordinary courage
and selflessness displayed by Capt. Fritz,
at the repeated risk of his own life above
and beyond the call of duty, were in
keeping with the highest traditions
of the U.S. Army and reflect the greatest
credit upon himself, his unit, and the
Armed Forces.

## Hagemeister, Charles Chris

**Rank and organization:**
Specialist Fifth Class (then Sp4c.),
U.S. Army, Headquarters and
Headquarters Company, 1st Battalion,
5th Cavalry Division (Airmobile).
**Place and date:**
Binh Dinh Province, Republic of
Vietnam, 20 March 1967.
**Entered service at:**
Lincoln, Nebr.
**Born:**
21 August 1946, Lincoln, Nebr.

**Citation:**
For conspicuous gallantry and intrepidity
in action at the risk of his life above and
beyond the call of duty. While
conducting combat operations against a
hostile force, Sp5c. Hagemeister's
platoon suddenly came under heavy
attack from 3 sides by an enemy force
occupying well concealed, fortified
positions and supported by machine-guns
and mortars. Seeing 2 of his comrades
seriously wounded in the initial action,

Sp5c. Hagemeister unhesitatingly and with total disregard for his safety, raced through the deadly hail of enemy fire to provide them medical aid. Upon learning that the platoon leader and several other soldiers also had been wounded, Sp5c. Hagemeister continued to brave the withering enemy fire and crawled forward to render lifesaving treatment and to offer words of encouragement. Attempting to evacuate the seriously wounded soldiers, Sp5c. Hagemeister was taken under fire at close range by an enemy sniper. Realizing that the lives of his fellow soldiers depended on his actions, Sp5c. Hagemeister seized a rifle from a fallen comrade, killed the sniper and 3 other enemy soldiers who were attempting to encircle his position, and silenced an enemy machine-gun that covered the area with deadly fire. Unable to remove the wounded to a less exposed location and aware of the enemy's efforts to isolate his unit, he dashed through the fusillade of fire to secure help from a nearby platoon. Returning with help, he placed men in positions to cover his advance as he moved to evacuate the wounded forward of his location. These efforts successfully completed, he then moved to the other flank and evacuated additional wounded men despite the fact that his every move drew fire from the enemy. Sp5c. Hagemeister's repeated heroic and selfless actions at the risk of his life saved the lives of many of his comrades and inspired their actions in repelling the enemy assault. Sp5c. Hagemeister's indomitable courage was in the highest traditions of the U.S. Armed Forces and reflect great credit upon himself.

## Hernandez, Rodolfo P.

**Rank and organization:**
Corporal, U.S. Army, Company G, 187th Airborne Regimental Combat Team.
**Place and date:**
Near Wontong-ni, Korea, 31 May 1951.
**Entered service at:**
Fowler, Calif.
**Born:**
14 April 1931, Colton, Calif.
**G.O. No.:**
40, 21 April 1962.

**Citation:**
Cpl. Hernandez, a member of Company G, distinguished himself by conspicuous gallantry and intrepidity above and beyond the call of duty in action against the enemy. His platoon, in defensive positions on Hill 420, came under ruthless attack by a numerically superior and fanatical hostile force, accompanied by heavy artillery, mortar, and machine-gun fire which inflicted numerous casualties on the platoon. His comrades were forced to withdraw due to lack of ammunition but Cpl. Hernandez, although wounded in an exchange of grenades, continued to deliver deadly fire into the ranks of the onrushing assailants until a ruptured cartridge rendered his rifle inoperative.

Immediately leaving his position, Cpl. Hernandez rushed the enemy armed only with rifle and bayonet. Fearlessly engaging the foe, he killed 6 of the enemy before falling unconscious from grenade, bayonet, and bullet wounds but his heroic action momentarily halted the enemy advance and enabled his unit to counterattack and retake the lost ground. The indomitable fighting spirit, outstanding courage, and tenacious devotion to duty clearly demonstrated by Cpl. Hernandez reflect the highest credit upon himself, the infantry, and the U.S. Army.

## Howard, Robert L.

**Rank and organization:**
First Lieutenant, U.S. Army, 5th Special Forces Group (Airborne), 1st Special Forces.
**Place and date:**
Republic of Vietnam, 30 December 1968.
**Entered service at:**
Montgomery, Ala.
**Born:**
11 July 1939, Opelika, Ala.

**Citation:**
For conspicuous gallantry and intrepidity in action at the risk of his life above and beyond the call of duty. 1st Lt. Howard (then Sfc.), distinguished himself while

serving as platoon sergeant of an American-Vietnamese platoon which was on a mission to rescue a missing American soldier in enemy controlled territory in the Republic of Vietnam. The platoon had left its helicopter landing zone and was moving out on its mission when it was attacked by an estimated 2-company force. During the initial engagement, 1st Lt. Howard was wounded and his weapon destroyed by a grenade explosion. 1st Lt. Howard saw his platoon leader had been wounded seriously and was exposed to fire. Although unable to walk, and weaponless, 1st Lt. Howard unhesitatingly crawled through a hail of fire to retrieve his wounded leader. As 1st Lt. Howard was administering first aid and removing the officer's equipment, an enemy bullet struck 1 of the ammunition pouches on the lieutenant's belt, detonating several magazines of ammunition. 1st Lt. Howard momentarily sought cover and then realizing that he must rejoin the platoon, which had been disorganized by the enemy attack, he again began dragging the seriously wounded officer toward the platoon area. Through his outstanding example of indomitable courage and bravery, 1st Lt. Howard was able to rally the platoon into an organized defense force. With complete disregard for his safety, 1st Lt. Howard crawled from position to position, administering first aid to the wounded, giving encouragement to the defenders and directing their fire on the encircling enemy. For 3-1/2 hours 1st Lt. Howard's small force and supporting aircraft successfully repulsed enemy attacks and finally were in sufficient control to permit the landing of rescue helicopters. 1st Lt. Howard personally supervised the loading of his men and did not leave the bullet-swept landing zone until all were aboard safely. 1st Lt. Howard's gallantry in action, his complete devotion to the welfare of his men at the risk of his life were in keeping with the highest traditions of the military service and reflect great credit on himself, his unit, and the U.S. Army.

## Ingman, Einar H., Jr.

**Rank and organization:**
Sergeant (then Cpl.), U.S. Army, Company E, 17th Infantry Regiment, 7th Infantry Division.
**Place and date:**
Near Maltari, Korea, 26 February 1951.
**Entered service at:**
Tomahawk, Wis.
**Born:**
6 October 1929, Milwaukee, Wis.
**G.O. No.:**
68, 2 August 1951.

**Citation:**
Sgt. Ingman, a member of Company E, distinguished himself by conspicuous gallantry and intrepidity above and beyond the call of duty in action against the enemy. The 2 leading squads of the assault platoon of his company, while attacking a strongly fortified ridge held by the enemy, were pinned down by withering fire and both squad leaders and several men were wounded. Cpl. Ingman assumed command, reorganized and combined the 2 squads, then moved from 1 position to another, designating fields of fire and giving advice and encouragement to the men. Locating an enemy machine-gun position that was raking his men with devastating fire he charged it alone, threw a grenade into the position, and killed the remaining crew with rifle fire. Another enemy machine-gun opened fire approximately 15 yards away and inflicted additional casualties to the group and stopped the attack. When Cpl. Ingman charged the second position he was hit by grenade fragments and a hail of fire which seriously wounded him about the face and neck and knocked him to the ground. With incredible courage and stamina, he arose instantly and, using only his rifle, killed the entire guncrew before falling unconscious from his wounds. As a result of the singular action by Cpl. Ingman the defense of the enemy was broken, his squad secured its objective and more than 100 hostile troops abandoned their weapons and fled in disorganized retreat. Cpl. Ingman's indomitable courage, extraordinary heroism, and superb leadership reflect the highest credit on himself and are in keeping with the esteemed traditions of the infantry and the U.S. Army.

## Keller, Leonard B.

**Rank and organization:**
Sergeant, U.S. Army, Company A,
3d Battalion, 60th Infantry,
9th Infantry Division.
**Place and date:**
Ap Bac Zone, Republic of Vietnam,
2 May 1967.
**Entered service at:**
Chicago, Ill.
**Born:**
25 February 1947, Rockford, Ill.

**Citation:**
For conspicuous gallantry and intrepidity in action at the risk of his life above and beyond the call of duty. Sweeping through an area where an enemy ambush had occurred earlier, Sgt. Keller's unit suddenly came under intense automatic weapons and small-arms fire from a number of enemy bunkers and numerous snipers in nearby trees. Sgt. Keller quickly moved to a position where he could fire at a bunker from which automatic fire was received, killing 1 Viet Cong who attempted to escape. Leaping to the top of a dike, he and a comrade charged the enemy bunkers, dangerously exposing themselves to the enemy fire. Armed with a light machine-gun, Sgt. Keller and his comrade began a systematic assault on the enemy bunkers. While Sgt. Keller neutralized the fire from the first bunker with his machine-gun, the other soldier charged a second bunker, killing its occupant. A third bunker contained an automatic rifleman who had pinned down much of the friendly platoon. Again, with utter disregard for the fire directed to them, the 2 men charged, killing the enemy within. Continuing their attack, Sgt. Keller and his comrade assaulted 4 more bunkers, killing the enemy within. During their furious assault, Sgt. Keller and his comrade had been almost continuously exposed to intense sniper fire as the enemy desperately sought to stop their attack. The ferocity of their assault had carried the soldiers beyond the line of bunkers into the treeline, forcing snipers to flee. The 2 men gave immediate chase, driving the enemy away from the friendly unit. When his ammunition was exhausted, Sgt. Keller returned to the platoon to assist in the evacuation of the wounded. The 2-man assault had driven an enemy platoon from a well prepared position, accounted for numerous enemy dead, and prevented further friendly casualties. Sgt. Keller's selfless heroism and indomitable fighting spirit saved the lives of many of his comrades and inflicted serious damage on the enemy. His acts were in keeping with the highest traditions of the military service and reflect great credit upon himself and the U.S. Army.

## Lee, Howard V.

**Rank and organization:**
Major, U.S. Marine Corps, Company E,
2d Battalion, 4th Marines, 3d Marine
Division (Rein).
**Place and date:**
Near Cam Lo, Republic of Vietnam,
8 and 9 August 1966.
**Entered service at:**
Dumfries, Va.
**Born:**
1 August 1933, New York, N.Y.

**Citation:**
For conspicuous gallantry and intrepidity at the risk of his life above and beyond the call of duty. A platoon of Maj. (then Capt.) Lee's company, while on an operation deep in enemy territory, was attacked and surrounded by a large Vietnamese force. Realizing that the unit had suffered numerous casualties, depriving it of effective leadership, and fully aware that the platoon was even then under heavy attack by the enemy, Maj. Lee took 7 men and proceeded by helicopter to reinforce the beleaguered platoon. Maj. Lee disembarked from the helicopter with 2 of his men and, braving withering enemy fire, led them into the perimeter, where he fearlessly moved from position to position, directing and encouraging the overtaxed troops. The enemy then launched a massive attack with the full might of their forces. Although painfully wounded by fragments from an enemy grenade in

several areas of his body, including his eye, Maj. Lee continued undauntedly throughout the night to direct the valiant defense, coordinate supporting fire, and apprise higher headquarters of the plight of the platoon. The next morning he collapsed from his wounds and was forced to relinquish command. However, the small band of marines had held their position and repeatedly fought off many vicious enemy attacks for a grueling 6 hours until their evacuation was effected the following morning. Maj. Lee's actions saved his men from capture, minimized the loss of lives, and dealt the enemy a severe defeat. His indomitable fighting spirit, superb leadership, and great personal valor in the face of tremendous odds, reflect great credit upon himself and are in keeping with the highest traditions of the Marine Corps and the U.S. Naval Service.

## Littrell, Gary Lee

**Rank and organization:**
Sergeant First Class, U.S. Army, Advisory Team 21, II Corps Advisory Group.
**Place and date:**
Kontum Province, Republic of Vietnam, 4-8 April 1970.
**Entered service at:**
Los Angeles, Calif.
**Born:**
26 October 1944, Henderson, Ky.

**Citation:**
For conspicuous gallantry and intrepidity in action at the risk of his life above and beyond the call of duty. Sfc. Littrell, U.S. Military Assistance Command, Vietnam, Advisory Team 21, distinguished himself while serving as a Light Weapons Infantry Advisor with the 23d Battalion, 2d Ranger Group, Republic of Vietnam Army, near Dak Seang. After establishing a defensive perimeter on a hill on April 4, the battalion was subjected to an intense enemy mortar attack which killed the Vietnamese commander, 1 advisor, and seriously wounded all the advisors except Sfc. Littrell. During the ensuing 4 days, Sfc. Littrell exhibited near superhuman endurance as he single-handedly bolstered the besieged battalion. Repeatedly abandoning positions of relative safety, he directed artillery and air support by day and marked the unit's location by night, despite the heavy, concentrated enemy fire. His dauntless will instilled in the men of the 23d Battalion a deep desire to resist. Assault after assault was repulsed as the battalion responded to the extraordinary leadership and personal example exhibited by Sfc. Littrell as he continuously moved to those points most seriously threatened by the enemy, redistributed ammunition, strengthened faltering defense, cared for the wounded and shouted encouragement to the Vietnamese in their own language. When the beleaguered battalion was finally ordered to withdraw, numerous ambushes were encountered. Sfc. Littrell repeatedly prevented widespread disorder by directing air strikes to within 50 meters of their position. Through his indomitable courage and complete disregard for his safety, he averted excessive loss of life and injury to the members of the battalion. The sustained extraordinary courage and selflessness displayed by Sfc. Littrell over an extended period of time were in keeping with the highest traditions of the military service and reflect great credit on him and the U.S. Army.

## Logan, James M.

**Rank and organization:**
Sergeant, U.S. Army, 36th Infantry Division.
**Place and date:**
Near Salerno, Italy, 9 September 1943.
**Entered service at:**
Luling, Tex.
**Birth:**
McNeil, Tex.
**G.O. No.:**
54, 5 July 1944.

**Citation:**
For conspicuous gallantry and intrepidity at risk of life above and beyond the call of duty in action involving actual conflict on 9 September 1943 in the vicinity of Salerno, Italy. As a rifleman of an infantry company, Sgt. Logan landed with the first wave of the assault echelon on the beaches of the Gulf of Salerno,

and after his company had advanced 800 yards inland and taken positions along the forward bank of an irrigation canal, the enemy began a serious counterattack from positions along a rock wall which ran parallel with the canal about 200 yards further inland. Voluntarily exposing himself to the fire of a machine-gun located along the rock wall, which sprayed the ground so close to him that he was splattered with dirt and rock splinters from the impact of the bullets, Sgt. Logan killed the first 3 Germans as they came through a gap in the wall. He then attacked the machine-gun. As he dashed across the 200 yards of exposed terrain, a withering stream of fire followed his advance. Reaching the wall, he crawled along the base, within easy reach of the enemy crouched along the opposite side, until he reached the gun. Jumping up, he shot the 2 gunners down, hurdled the wall, and seized the gun. Swinging it around, he immediately opened fire on the enemy with the remaining ammunition, raking their flight and inflicting further casualties on them as they fled. After smashing the machine-gun over the rocks, Sgt. Logan captured an enemy officer and private who were attempting to sneak away. Later in the morning, Sgt. Logan went after a sniper hidden in a house about 150 yards from the company. Again the intrepid Sgt. Logan ran a gauntlet of fire to reach his objective. Shooting the lock off the door,

Sgt. Logan kicked it in and shot the sniper who had just reached the bottom of the stairs. The conspicuous gallantry and intrepidity which characterized St. Logan's exploits proved a constant inspiration to all the men of his company, and aided materially in insuring the success of the beachhead at Salerno.

## Lynch, Allen James

**Rank and organization:**
Sergeant, U.S. Army, Company D, 1st Battalion (Airmobile), 12th Cavalry, 1st Cavalry Division (Airmobile).
**Place and date:**
Near My An (2), Binh Dinh Province, Republic of Vietnam, 15 December 1967.
**Entered service at:**
Chicago, Ill.
**Born:**
28 October 1945, Chicago, Ill.

**Citation:**
For conspicuous gallantry and intrepidity in action at the risk of his life above and beyond the call of duty. Sgt. Lynch (then Sp4c.) distinguished himself while serving as a radio telephone operator with Company D. While serving in the forward element on an operation near the village of My An, his unit became heavily engaged with a numerically superior enemy force. Quickly and accurately assessing the situation, Sgt. Lynch provided his commander with information which subsequently proved

essential to the unit's successful actions. Observing 3 wounded comrades lying exposed to enemy fire, Sgt. Lynch dashed across 50 meters of open ground through a withering hail of enemy fire to administer aid. Reconnoitering a nearby trench for a covered position to protect the wounded from intense hostile fire, he killed 2 enemy soldiers at point blank range. With the trench cleared, he unhesitatingly returned to the fire-swept area 3 times to carry the wounded men to safety. When his company was forced to withdraw by the superior firepower of the enemy, Sgt. Lynch remained to aid his comrades at the risk of his life rather than abandon them. Alone, he defended his isolated position for 2 hours against the advancing enemy. Using only his rifle and a grenade, he stopped them just short of his trench, killing 5. Again, disregarding his safety in the face of withering hostile fire, he crossed 70 meters of exposed terrain 5 times to carry his wounded comrades to a more secure area. Once he had assured their comfort and safety, Sgt. Lynch located the counterattacking friendly company to assist in directing the attack and evacuating the 3 casualties. His gallantry at the risk of his life is in the highest traditions of the military service, Sgt. Lynch has reflected great credit on himself, the 12th Cavalry, and the U.S. Army.

## Miller, Franklin D.

**Rank and organization:**
Staff Sergeant, U.S. Army, 5th Special Forces Group, 1st Special Forces.
**Place and date:**
Kontum Province, Republic of Vietnam, 5 January 1970.
**Entered service at:**
Albuquerque, N. Mex.
**Born:**
27 January 1945, Elizabeth City, N.C.

**Citation:**
For conspicuous gallantry and intrepidity in action at the risk of his life above and beyond the call of duty. S/Sgt. Miller, 5th Special Forces Group, distinguished himself while serving as team leader of an American-Vietnamese long-range reconnaissance patrol operating deep within enemy controlled territory. Leaving the helicopter insertion point, the patrol moved forward on its mission. Suddenly, 1 of the team members tripped a hostile boobytrap which wounded 4 soldiers. S/Sgt. Miller, knowing that the explosion would alert the enemy, quickly administered first aid to the wounded and directed the team into positions across a small stream bed at the base of a steep hill. Within a few minutes, S/Sgt. Miller saw the lead element of what he estimated to be a platoon-size enemy force moving toward his location. Concerned for the safety of his men, he directed the small team to move up the hill to a more secure position.

He remained alone, separated from the patrol, to meet the attack. S/Sgt. Miller single-handedly repulsed 2 determined attacks by the numerically superior enemy force and caused them to withdraw in disorder. He rejoined his team, established contact with a forward air controller and arranged the evacuation of his patrol. However, the only suitable extraction location in the heavy jungle was a bomb crater some 150 meters from the team location. S/Sgt. Miller reconnoitered the route to the crater and led his men through the enemy controlled jungle to the extraction site. As the evacuation helicopter hovered over the crater to pick up the patrol, the enemy launched a savage automatic weapon and rocket-propelled grenade attack against the beleaguered team, driving off the rescue helicopter. S/Sgt. Miller led the team in a valiant defense which drove back the enemy in its attempt to overrun the small patrol. Although seriously wounded and with every man in his patrol a casualty, S/Sgt. Miller moved forward to again single-handedly meet the hostile attackers. From his forward exposed position, S/Sgt. Miller gallantly repelled 2 attacks by the enemy before a friendly relief force reached the patrol location. S/Sgt. Miller's gallantry, intrepidity in action, and selfless devotion to the welfare of his comrades are in keeping with the highest traditions of the military service and reflect great credit on him, his unit, and the U.S. Army.

## Millett, Lewis L.

**Rank and organization:**
Captain, U.S. Army, Company E, 27th Infantry Regiment.
**Place and date:**
Vicinity of Soam-Ni, Korea, 7 February 1951.
**Entered service at:**
Mechanic Falls, Maine.
**Born:**
15 December 1920, Mechanic Falls, Maine.
**G.O. No.:**
69, 2 August 1951.

**Citation:**
Capt. Millett, Company E, distinguished himself by conspicuous gallantry and intrepidity above and beyond the call of duty in action. While personally leading his company in an attack against a strongly held position he noted that the 1st Platoon was pinned down by small-arms, automatic, and antitank fire. Capt. Millett ordered the 3d Platoon forward, placed himself at the head of the 2 platoons, and, with fixed bayonet, led the assault up the fire-swept hill. In the fierce charge Capt. Millett bayoneted 2 enemy soldiers and boldly continued on, throwing grenades, clubbing and bayoneting the enemy, while urging his men forward by shouting encouragement. Despite vicious opposing fire, the whirlwind hand-to-hand assault carried to the crest of the hill. His dauntless leadership and personal courage so inspired his men that they stormed into

the hostile position and used their bayonets with such lethal effect that the enemy fled in wild disorder. During this fierce onslaught Capt. Millett was wounded by grenade fragments but refused evacuation until the objective was taken and firmly secured. The superb leadership, conspicuous courage, and consummate devotion to duty demonstrated by Capt. Millett were directly responsible for the successful accomplishment of a hazardous mission and reflect the highest credit on himself and the heroic traditions of the military service.

## Modrzejewski, Robert J.

**Rank and organization:**
Major (then Capt.), U.S. Marine Corps, Company K, 3d Battalion, 4th Marines, 3d Marine Division, FMF.
**Place and date:**
Republic of Vietnam, 15 to 18 July 1966.
**Entered service at:**
Milwaukee, Wis.
**Born:**
3 July 1934, Milwaukee, Wis.

**Citation:**
For conspicuous gallantry and intrepidity at the risk of his life above and beyond the call of duty. On 15 July, during Operation HASTINGS, Company K was landed in an enemy-infested jungle area

to establish a blocking position at a major enemy trail network. Shortly after landing, the company encountered a reinforced enemy platoon in a well-organized, defensive position. Maj. Modrzejewski led his men in the successful seizure of the enemy redoubt, which contained large quantities of ammunition and supplies. That evening, a numerically superior enemy force counterattacked in an effort to retake the vital supply area, thus setting the pattern of activity for the next 2-1/2 days. In the first series of attacks, the enemy assaulted repeatedly in overwhelming numbers but each time was repulsed by the gallant marines. The second night, the enemy struck in battalion strength, and Maj. Modrzejewski was wounded in this intensive action which was fought at close quarters. Although exposed to enemy fire, and despite his painful wounds, he crawled 200 meters to provide critical needed ammunition to an exposed element of his command and was constantly present wherever the fighting was heaviest, despite numerous casualties, a dwindling supply of ammunition and the knowledge that they were surrounded, he skillfully directed artillery fire to within a few meters of his position and courageously inspired the efforts of his company in repelling the aggressive enemy attack. On 18 July, Company K was attacked by a regimental-size enemy force. Although his unit was vastly outnumbered and weakened by the previous fighting, Maj. Modrzejewski reorganized his men and calmly moved among them to encourage and direct their efforts to heroic limits as they fought to overcome

the vicious enemy onslaught. Again he called in air and artillery strikes at close range with devastating effect on the enemy, which together with the bold and determined fighting of the men of Company K, repulsed the fanatical attack of the larger North Vietnamese force. His unparalleled personal heroism and indomitable leadership inspired his men to a significant victory over the enemy force and reflected great credit upon himself, the Marine Corps, and the U.S. Naval Service.

## Montgomery, Jack C.

**Rank and organization:**
First Lieutenant, U.S. Army, 45th Infantry Division.
**Place and date:**
Near Padiglione, Italy, 22 February 1944.
**Entered service at:**
Sallisaw, Okla.
**Birth:**
Long, Okla.
**G.O. No.:**
5, 15 January 1945.

**Citation:**
For conspicuous gallantry and intrepidity at risk of life above and beyond the call of duty on 22 February 1944, near Padiglione, Italy. Two hours before daybreak a strong force of enemy infantry established themselves in 3 echelons at 50 yards, 100 yards, and 300 yards, respectively, in front of

the rifle platoons commanded by 1st Lt. Montgomery. The closest position, consisting of 4 machine-guns and 1 mortar, threatened the immediate security of the platoon position. Seizing an M1 rifle and several handgrenades, 1st Lt. Montgomery crawled up a ditch to within handgrenade range of the enemy. Then climbing boldly onto a little mound, he fired his rifle and threw his grenades so accurately that he killed 8 of the enemy and captured the remaining 4. Returning to his platoon, he called for artillery fire on a house, in and around which he suspected that the majority of the enemy had entrenched themselves. Arming himself with a carbine, he proceeded along the shallow ditch, as withering fire from the riflemen and machine-gunners in the second position was concentrated on him. He attacked this position with such fury that 7 of the enemy surrendered to him, and both machine-guns were silenced. Three German dead were found in the vicinity later that morning. 1st Lt. Montgomery continued boldly toward the house, 300 yards from his platoon position. It was now daylight, and the enemy observation was excellent across the flat open terrain which lead to 1st Lt. Montgomery's objective. When the artillery barrage had lifted, 1st Lt. Montgomery ran fearlessly toward the strongly defended position. As the

enemy started streaming out of the house, 1st Lt. Montgomery, unafraid of treacherous snipers, exposed himself daringly to assemble the surrendering enemy and send them to the rear. His fearless, aggressive, and intrepid actions that morning, accounted for a total of 11 enemy dead, 32 prisoners, and an unknown number of wounded. That night, while aiding an adjacent unit to repulse a counterattack, he was struck by mortar fragments and seriously wounded. The selflessness and courage exhibited by 1st Lt. Montgomery in alone attacking 3 strong enemy positions inspired his men to a degree beyond estimation.

## Murray, Charles P., Jr.

**Rank and organization:**
First Lieutenant, U.S. Army, Company C, 30th Infantry, 3d Infantry Division.
**Place and date:**
Near Kaysersberg, France, 16 December 1944.
**Entered service at:**
Wilmington, N.C.
**Birth:**
Baltimore, Md.
**G.O. No.:**
63, 1 August 1945.

**Citation:**
For commanding Company C, 30th Infantry, displaying supreme courage and heroic initiative near Kaysersberg, France, on 16 December 1944, while leading a reinforced platoon into enemy territory. Descending into a

valley beneath hilltop positions held by our troops, he observed a force of 200 Germans pouring deadly mortar, bazooka, machine-gun, and small arms fire into an American battalion occupying the crest of the ridge. The enemy's position in a sunken road, though hidden from the ridge, was open to a flank attack by 1st Lt. Murray's patrol but he hesitated to commit so small a force to battle with the superior and strongly disposed enemy. Crawling out ahead of his troops to a vantage point, he called by radio for artillery fire. His shells bracketed the German force, but when he was about to correct the range his radio went dead. He returned to his patrol, secured grenades and a rifle to launch them and went back to his self-appointed outpost. His first shots disclosed his position; the enemy directed heavy fire against him as he methodically fired his missiles into the narrow defile. Again he returned to his patrol. With an automatic rifle and ammunition, he once more moved to his exposed position. Burst after burst he fired into the enemy, killing 20, wounding many others, and completely disorganizing its ranks, which began to withdraw. He prevented the removal of 3 German mortars by knocking out a truck. By that time a mortar had been brought to his support. 1st Lt. Murray directed fire of this weapon, causing further casualties and confusion in the German ranks. Calling on his patrol to follow, he then moved out toward his original objective, possession of a bridge and construction of a roadblock. He captured 10 Germans in foxholes. An eleventh, while pretending to surrender, threw a grenade which knocked him to the ground, inflicting 8 wounds. Though suffering and bleeding profusely, he refused to return to the rear until he had chosen the spot for the block and had seen his men correctly deployed. By his single-handed attack on an overwhelming force and by his intrepid and heroic fighting, 1st Lt. Murray stopped a counterattack, established an advance position against formidable odds, and provided an inspiring example for the men of his command.

## Myers, Reginald R.

**Rank and organization:**
Major, U.S. Marine Corps, 3d Battalion, 1st Marines, 1st Marine Division, (Rein).
**Place and date:**
Near Hagaru-ri, Korea, 29 November 1950.
**Entered service at:**
Boise, Idaho.
**Born:**
26 November 1919, Boise, Idaho.

**Citation:**
For conspicuous gallantry and intrepidity at the risk of his life above and beyond the call of duty as executive officer of the 3d Battalion, in action against enemy aggressor forces. Assuming command of a composite unit of Army and Marine service and headquarters elements totaling approximately 250 men, during a critical stage in the vital defense of the strategically important military base at Hagaru-ri, Maj. Myers immediately initiated a determined and aggressive counterattack against a well-entrenched and cleverly concealed enemy force numbering an estimated 4,000. Severely handicapped by a lack of trained personnel and experienced leaders in his valiant efforts to regain maximum ground prior to daylight, he persisted in constantly exposing himself to intense, accurate, and sustained hostile fire in order to direct and supervise the employment of his men and to encourage and spur them on in pressing the attack. Inexorably moving forward up the steep, snow-covered slope with his depleted group in the face of apparently insurmountable odds, he concurrently directed artillery and mortar fire with superb skill and although losing 170 of his men during 14 hours of raging combat in subzero temperatures, continued to reorganize his unit and spearhead the attack which resulted in 600 enemy killed and 500 wounded. By his exceptional and valorous leadership throughout, Maj. Myers contributed directly to the success of his unit in restoring the perimeter. His resolute spirit of self-sacrifice and unfaltering devotion to duty enhance and sustain the highest traditions of the U.S. Naval Service.

## Novosel, Michael J.

**Rank and organization:**
Chief Warrant Officer, U.S. Army, 82d Medical Detachment, 45th Medical Company, 68th Medical Group.
**Place and date:**
Kien Tuong Province, Republic of Vietnam, 2 October 1969.
**Entered service at:**
Kenner, La.
**Born:**
3 September 1922, Etna, Pa.

**Citation:**
For conspicuous gallantry and intrepidity in action at the risk of his life above and beyond the call of duty. CWO Novosel, 82d Medical Detachment, distinguished himself while serving as commander of a medical evacuation helicopter. He unhesitatingly maneuvered his helicopter into a heavily fortified and defended enemy training area where a group of wounded Vietnamese soldiers were pinned down by a large enemy force. Flying without gunship or other cover and exposed to intense machine-gun fire, CWO Novosel was able to locate and rescue a wounded soldier. Since all communications with the beleaguered troops had been lost, he repeatedly circled the battle area, flying at low level under continuous heavy fire, to attract the attention of the scattered friendly troops. This display of courage visibly raised their morale, as they recognized

this as a signal to assemble for evacuation. On 6 occasions he and his crew were forced out of the battle area by the intense enemy fire, only to circle and return from another direction to land and extract additional troops. Near the end of the mission, a wounded soldier was spotted close to an enemy bunker. Fully realizing that he would attract a hail of enemy fire, CWO Novosel nevertheless attempted the extraction by hovering the helicopter backward. As the man was pulled on aboard, enemy automatic weapons opened fire at close range, damaged the aircraft and wounded CWO Novosel. He momentarily lost control of the aircraft, but quickly recovered and departed under the withering enemy fire. In all, 15 extremely hazardous extractions were performed in order to remove wounded personnel. As a direct result of his selfless conduct, the lives of 29 soldiers were saved. The extraordinary heroism displayed by CWO Novosel was an inspiration to his comrades in arms and reflect great credit on him, his unit, and the U.S. Army.

## O'Malley, Robert E.

**Rank and organization:**
Sergeant (then Cpl.), U.S. Marine Corps, Company I, 3d Battalion, 3d Marine Regiment, 3d Marine Division (Rein).

**Place and date:**
Near An Cu'ong 2, South Vietnam, 18 August 1965.
**Entered service at:**
New York, N.Y.
**Born:**
3 June 1943, New York, N.Y.

**Citation:**
For conspicuous gallantry and intrepidity in action against the communist (Viet Cong) forces at the risk of his life above and beyond the call of duty. While leading his squad in the assault against a strongly entrenched enemy force, his unit came under intense small-arms fire. With complete disregard for his personal safety, Sgt. O'Malley raced across an open rice paddy to a trench line where the enemy forces were located. Jumping into the trench, he attacked the Viet Cong with his rifle and grenades, and singly killed 8 of the enemy. He then led his squad to the assistance of an adjacent marine unit which was suffering heavy casualties. Continuing to press forward, he reloaded his weapon and fired with telling effect into the enemy emplacement. He personally assisted in the evacuation of several wounded marines, and again regrouping the remnants of his squad, he returned to the point of the heaviest fighting. Ordered to an evacuation point by an officer, Sgt. O'Malley gathered his besieged and badly wounded squad, and boldly led them under fire to a helicopter for withdrawal. Although 3 times wounded in this encounter, and facing imminent death from a fanatic and determined enemy, he steadfastly refused evacuation and continued to

cover his squad's boarding of the helicopters while, from an exposed position, he delivered fire against the enemy until his wounded men were evacuated. Only then, with his last mission accomplished, did he permit himself to be removed from the battlefield. By his valor, leadership, and courageous efforts in behalf of his comrades, he served as an inspiration to all who observed him, and reflected the highest credit upon the Marine Corps and the U.S. Naval Service.

## Paige, Mitchell

**Rank and organization:**
Platoon Sergeant, U.S. Marine Corps.
**Place and date:**
Solomon Islands, 26 October 1942.
**Entered service at:**
Pennsylvania.
**Born:**
31 August 1918, Charleroi, Pa.

**Citation:**
For extraordinary heroism and conspicuous gallantry in action above and beyond the call of duty while serving with a company of marines in combat against enemy Japanese forces in the Solomon Islands on 26 October 1942. When the enemy broke through the line directly in front of his position, P/Sgt. Paige, commanding a machine-gun section with fearless determination,

continued to direct the fire of his gunners until all his men were either killed or wounded. Alone, against the deadly hail of Japanese shells, he fought with his gun and when it was destroyed, took over another, moving from gun to gun, never ceasing his withering fire against the advancing hordes until reinforcements finally arrived. Then, forming a new line, he dauntlessly and aggressively led a bayonet charge, driving the enemy back and preventing a breakthrough in our lines. His great personal valor and unyielding devotion to duty were in keeping the highest traditions of the U.S. Naval Service.

## Patterson, Robert Martin

**Rank and organization:**
Sergeant, U.S. Army, Troop B, 2d Squadron, 17th Cavalry.
**Place and date:**
Near La Chu, Republic of Vietnam, 6 May 1968.
**Entered service at:**
Raleigh, N.C.
**Born:**
16 April 1948, Durham, N.C.

**Citation:**
For conspicuous gallantry and intrepidity in action at the risk of his life above and beyond the call of duty. Sgt. Patterson (then Sp4c.) distinguished himself while serving as a fire team leader of the 3d Platoon, Troop B, during an assault against a North Vietnamese Army battalion which was entrenched in a heavily fortified position. When the leading squad of the 3d Platoon was pinned down by heavy interlocking automatic weapon and rocket propelled grenade fire from 2 enemy bunkers, Sgt. Patterson and the 2 other members of his assault team moved forward under a hail of enemy fire to destroy the bunkers with grenade and machine-gun fire. Observing that his comrades were being fired on from a third enemy bunker covered by enemy gunners in 1-man spider holes, Sgt. Patterson, with complete disregard for his safety and ignoring the warning of his comrades that he was moving into a bunker complex, assaulted and destroyed the position. Although exposed to intensive small arm and grenade fire from the bunkers and their mutually supporting emplacements, Sgt. Patterson continued his assault upon the bunkers which were impeding the advance of his unit. Sgt. Patterson single-handedly destroyed by rifle and grenade fire 5 enemy bunkers, killed 8 enemy soldiers and captured 7 weapons. His dauntless courage and heroism inspired his platoon to resume the attack and to penetrate the enemy defensive position. Sgt. Patterson's action at the risk of his life has reflected great credit upon himself, his unit, and the U.S. Army.

## Pittman, Richard A.

**Rank and organization:**
Sergeant (then L/Cpl.), U.S. Marine Corps, Company I, 3d Battalion, 5th Marines, 1st Marine Division (Rein) FMF.
**Place and date:**
Near the Demilitarized Zone, Republic of Vietnam, 24 July 1966.
**Entered service at:**
Stockton, Calif.
**Born:**
26 May 1945, French Camp, San Joaquin, Calif.

**Citation:**
For conspicuous gallantry and intrepidity at the risk of his life above and beyond the call of duty. While Company I was conducting an operation along the axis of a narrow jungle trail, the leading company elements suffered numerous casualties when they suddenly came under heavy fire from a well concealed and numerically superior enemy force. Hearing the engaged marines' calls for more firepower, Sgt. Pittman quickly exchanged his rifle for a machine-gun and several belts of ammunition, left the relative safety of his platoon, and unhesitatingly rushed forward to aid his comrades. Taken under intense enemy small-arms fire at point blank range during his advance, he returned the fire, silencing the enemy position. As Sgt. Pittman continued to forge forward to aid members of the leading platoon, he again came under heavy fire from

2 automatic weapons which he promptly destroyed. Learning that there were additional wounded marines 50 yards further along the trail, he braved a withering hail of enemy mortar and small-arms fire to continue onward. As he reached the position where the leading marines had fallen, he was suddenly confronted with a bold frontal attack by 30 to 40 enemy. Totally disregarding his safety, he calmly established a position in the middle of the trail and raked the advancing enemy with devastating machine-gun fire. His weapon rendered ineffective, he picked up an enemy submachine-gun and, together with a pistol seized from a fallen comrade, continued his lethal fire until the enemy force had withdrawn. Having exhausted his ammunition except for a grenade which he hurled at the enemy, he then rejoined his platoon. Sgt. Pittman's daring initiative, bold fighting spirit and selfless devotion to duty inflicted many enemy casualties, disrupted the enemy attack and saved the lives of many of his wounded comrades. His personal valor at grave risk to himself reflects the highest credit upon himself, the Marine Corps, and the U.S. Naval Service.

## Pope, Everett Parker

**Rank and organization:**
Captain, U.S. Marine Corps, Company C, 1st Battalion, 1st Marines, 1st Marine Division.

**Place and date:**
Peleliu Island, Palau group, 19-20 September 1944.
**Entered service at:**
Massachusetts.
**Born:**
16 July 1919, Milton, Mass.

**Citation:**
For conspicuous gallantry and intrepidity at the risk of his life above and beyond the call of duty while serving as commanding officer of Company C, 1st Battalion, 1st Marines, 1st Marine Division, during action against enemy Japanese forces on Peleliu Island, Palau group, on 19-20 September 1944. Subjected to pointblank cannon fire which caused heavy casualties and badly disorganized his company while assaulting a steep coral hill, Capt. Pope rallied his men and gallantly led them to the summit in the face of machine-gun, mortar, and sniper fire. Forced by widespread hostile attack to deploy the remnants of his company thinly in order to hold the ground won, and with his machine-guns out of order and insufficient water and ammunition, he remained on the exposed hill with 12 men and 1 wounded officer, determined to hold through the night. Attacked continuously with grenades, machine-guns, and rifles from 3 sides, he and his valiant men fiercely beat back or destroyed the enemy, resorting to hand-to-hand combat as the supply of ammunition dwindled, and still maintaining his lines with his 8 remaining riflemen when daylight brought more deadly fire and he was ordered to withdraw. His valiant

leadership against devastating odds while protecting the units below from heavy Japanese attack reflects the highest credit upon Capt. Pope and the U.S. Naval Service.

## Ray, Ronald Eric

**Rank and organization:**
Captain (then 1st Lt.), U.S. Army, Company A, 2d Battalion, 35th Infantry, 25th Infantry Division.
**Place and date:**
La Drang Valley, Republic of Vietnam, 19 June 1966.
**Entered service at:**
Atlanta, Ga.
**Born:**
7 December 1941, Cordelle, Ga.

**Citation:**
For conspicuous gallantry and intrepidity in action at the risk of his life above and beyond the call of duty. Capt. Ray distinguished himself while serving as a platoon leader with Company A. When 1 of his ambush patrols was attacked by an estimated reinforced Viet Cong company, Capt. Ray organized a reaction force and quickly moved through 2 kilometers of mountainous jungle terrain to the contact area. After breaking through the hostile lines to reach the beleaguered patrol, Capt. Ray began

directing the reinforcement of the site. When an enemy position pinned down 3 of his men with a heavy volume of automatic weapons fire, he silenced the emplacement with a grenade and killed 4 Viet Cong with his rifle fire. As medics were moving a casualty toward a sheltered position, they began receiving intense hostile fire. While directing suppressive fire on the enemy position, Capt. Ray moved close enough to silence the enemy with a grenade. A few moments later Capt. Ray saw an enemy grenade land, unnoticed, near 2 of his men. Without hesitation or regard for his safety he dove between the grenade and the men, thus shielding them from the explosion while receiving wounds in his exposed feet and legs. He immediately sustained additional wounds in his legs from an enemy machine-gun, but nevertheless he silenced the emplacement with another grenade. Although suffering great pain from his wounds, Capt. Ray continued to direct his men, providing the outstanding courage and leadership they vitally needed, and prevented their annihilation by successfully leading them from their surrounded position. Only after assuring that his platoon was no longer in immediate danger did he allow himself to be evacuated for medical treatment. By his gallantry at the risk of his life in the highest traditions of the military service, Capt. Ray has reflected great credit on himself, his unit, and the U.S. Army.

## Rocco, Louis R.

**Rank and organization:**
Warrant Officer (then Sergeant First Class), U.S. Army, Advisory Team 162, U.S. Military Assistance Command.
**Place and date:**
Northeast of Katum, Republic of Vietnam, 24 May 1970.
**Entered service at:**
Los Angeles, Calif.
**Born:**
19 November 1938,
Albuquerque, N. Mex.

**Citation:**
WO Rocco distinguished himself when he volunteered to accompany a medical evacuation team on an urgent mission to evacuate 8 critically wounded Army of the Republic of Vietnam personnel. As the helicopter approached the landing zone, it became the target for intense enemy automatic weapons fire. Disregarding his own safety, WO Rocco identified and placed accurate suppressive fire on the enemy positions as the aircraft descended toward the landing zone. Sustaining major damage from the enemy fire, the aircraft was forced to crash land, causing WO Rocco to sustain a fractured wrist and hip and severely bruised back. Ignoring his injuries, he extracted the survivors from the burning wreckage, sustaining burns to his own body. Despite intense enemy fire, WO Rocco carried each unconscious man across approximately 20 meters of exposed terrain to the Army of the Republic of Vietnam perimeter. On each trip, his severely burned hands and broken wrist caused excruciating pain, but the lives of the unconscious crash survivors were more important than his personal discomfort, and he continued his rescue efforts. Once inside the friendly position, WO Rocco helped administer first aid to his wounded comrades until his wounds and burns caused him to collapse and lose consciousness. His bravery under fire and intense devotion to duty were directly responsible for saving 3 of his fellow soldiers from certain death. His unparalleled bravery in the face of enemy fire, his complete disregard for his own pain and injuries, and his performance were far above and beyond the call of duty and were in keeping with the highest traditions of self-sacrifice and courage of the military service.

## Rosser, Ronald E.

**Rank and organization:**
Corporal, U.S. Army, Heavy Mortar Company, 38th Infantry Regiment, 2d Infantry Division.
**Place and date:**
Vicinity of Ponggilli, Korea, 12 January 1952.
**Entered service at:**
Crooksville, Ohio.
**Born:**
24 October 1929, Columbus, Ohio.
**G.O. No.:**
67, 7 July 1952.

Cpl. Rosser distinguished himself by conspicuous gallantry above and beyond the call of duty. While assaulting heavily fortified enemy hill positions, Company L, 38th Infantry Regiment, was stopped by fierce automatic-weapons, small arms, artillery, and mortar fire. Cpl. Rosser, a forward observer, was with the lead platoon of Company L when it came under fire from 2 directions. Cpl. Rosser turned his radio over to his assistant and, disregarding the enemy fire, charged the enemy positions armed with only carbine and a grenade. At the first bunker, he silenced its occupants with a burst from his weapon. Gaining the top of the hill, he killed 2 enemy soldiers, and then went down the trench, killing 5 more as he advanced. He then hurled his grenade into a bunker and shot 2 other soldiers as they emerged. Having exhausted his ammunition, he returned through the enemy fire to obtain more ammunition and grenades and charged the hill once more. Calling on others to follow him, he assaulted 2 more enemy bunkers. Although those who attempted to join him became casualties, Cpl. Rosser once again exhausted his ammunition, obtained a new supply, and returning to the hilltop a third time, hurled grenades into the enemy positions. During this heroic action Cpl. Rosser single-handedly killed at least 13 of the enemy. After exhausting his ammunition he accompanied the withdrawing platoon, and though himself wounded, made several trips across open terrain still under enemy fire to help remove other men injured more seriously than himself. This outstanding soldier's courageous and selfless devotion to duty is worthy of emulation by all men. He has contributed magnificently to the high traditions of the military service.

## Sitter, Carl L.

**Rank and organization:**
Captain, U.S. Marine Corps, Company G, 3d Battalion, 1st Marine, 1st Marine Division (Rein).
**Place and date:**
Hagaru-ri, Korea, 29 and 30 November 1950.
**Entered service at:**
Pueblo, Colo.
**Born:**
2 December 1921, Syracuse, Mo.

**Citation:**
For conspicuous gallantry and intrepidity at the risk of his life above and beyond the call of duty as commanding officer of Company G, in action against enemy aggressor forces. Ordered to break through enemy-infested territory to reinforce his battalion the morning of 29 November, Capt. Sitter continuously exposed himself to enemy fire as he led his company forward and, despite 25 percent casualties suffered in the furious action, succeeded in driving through to his objective. Assuming the responsibility of attempting to seize and occupy a strategic area occupied by a hostile force of regiment strength deeply entrenched on a snow-covered hill commanding the entire valley southeast of the town, as well as the line of march of friendly troops withdrawing to the south, he reorganized his depleted units the following morning and boldly led them up the steep, frozen hillside under blistering fire, encouraging and redeploying his troops as casualties occurred and directing forward platoons as they continued the drive to the top of the ridge. During the night when a vastly outnumbering enemy launched a sudden, vicious counterattack, setting the hill ablaze with mortar, machine-gun, and automatic-weapons fire and taking a heavy toll in troops, Capt. Sitter visited each foxhole and gun position, coolly deploying and integrating reinforcing units consisting of service personnel unfamiliar with infantry tactics into a coordinated combat team and instilling in every man the will and determination to hold his position at all cost. With the enemy penetrating his lines in repeated counterattacks which often required hand to hand combat, and, on one occasion infiltrating to the command post with handgrenades, he fought gallantly with his men in repulsing and killing the fanatic attackers in each encounter. Painfully wounded in the face, arms, and chest by bursting grenades, he staunchly refused to be evacuated and continued to fight on until a successful defense of the area was assured with a loss to the enemy of more that 50 percent dead, wounded, and captured. His valiant

leadership, superb tactics, and great personal valor throughout 36 hours of bitter combat reflect the highest credit upon Capt. Sitter and the U.S. Naval Service.

## Swett, James Elms

**Rank and organization:**
First Lieutenant, U.S. Marine Corps Reserve, Marine Fighting Squadron 221, with Marine Aircraft Group 12, 1st Marine Aircraft Wing.
**Place and date:**
Solomon Islands area, 7 April 1943.
**Entered service at:**
California.
**Born:**
15 June 1920, Seattle, Wash.
**Other Navy award:**
Distinguished Flying Cross with 1 Gold Star.

**Citation:**
For extraordinary heroism and personal valor above and beyond the call of duty, as division leader of Marine Fighting Squadron 221 with Marine Aircraft Group 12, 1st Marine Aircraft Wing, in action against enemy Japanese aerial forces in the Solomon Islands area, 7 April 1943. In a daring fight to intercept a wave of 150 Japanese planes, 1st Lt. Swett unhesitatingly hurled his 4-plane division into action against a formation of 15 enemy bombers and personally exploded 3 hostile planes in midair with accurate and deadly fire during his dive. Although separated from his division while clearing the heavy concentration of antiaircraft fire, he boldly attacked 6 enemy bombers, engaged the first 4 in turn and, unaided, shot down all in flames. Exhausting his ammunition as he closed the fifth Japanese bomber, he relentlessly drove his attack against terrific opposition which partially disabled his engine, shattered the windscreen and slashed his face. In spite of this, he brought his battered plane down with skillful precision in the water off Tulagi without further injury. The superb airmanship and tenacious fighting spirit which enabled 1st Lt. Swett to destroy 7 enemy bombers in a single flight were in keeping with the highest traditions of the U.S. Naval Service.

## Taylor, James Allen

**Rank and organization:**
Captain (then 1st Lt.), U.S. Army, Troop B, 1st Cavalry, American Division.
**Place and date:**
West of Que Son, Republic of Vietnam, 9 November 1967.
**Entered service at:**
San Francisco, Calif.
**Born:**
31 December 1937, Arcata, Calif.

**Citation:**
Capt. Taylor, Armor, was serving as executive officer of Troop B, 1st Squadron. His troop was engaged in an attack on a fortified position west of Que Son when it came under intense enemy recoilless rifle, mortar, and automatic weapons fire from an enemy strong point located immediately to its front. One armored cavalry assault vehicle was hit immediately by recoilless rifle fire and all 5 crew members were wounded. Aware that the stricken vehicle was in grave danger of exploding, Capt. Taylor rushed forward and personally extracted the wounded to safety despite the hail of enemy fire and exploding ammunition. Within minutes a second armored cavalry assault vehicle was hit by multiple recoilless rifle rounds. Despite the continuing intense enemy fire, Capt. Taylor moved forward on foot to rescue the wounded men from the burning vehicle and personally removed all the crewmen to the safety of a nearby dike. Moments later the vehicle exploded. As he was returning to his vehicle, a bursting mortar round painfully wounded Capt. Taylor, yet he valiantly returned to his vehicle to relocate the medical evacuation landing zone to an area closer to the front lines. As he was moving his vehicle, it came under machine-gun fire from an enemy position not 50 yards away. Capt. Taylor engaged the position with his machine-gun, killing the 3-man crew. Upon arrival at the new evacuation site, still another vehicle was struck. Once again Capt. Taylor rushed forward and pulled the wounded from the vehicle, loaded

them aboard his vehicle, and returned them to safety to the evacuation site. His actions of unsurpassed valor were a source of inspiration to his entire troop, contributed significantly to the success of the overall assault on the enemy position, and were directly responsible for saving the lives of a number of his fellow soldiers. His actions were in keeping with the highest traditions of the military profession and reflect great credit upon himself, his unit, and the U.S. Army.

## Thornton, Michael Edwin

**Rank and organization:**
Petty Officer, U.S. Navy, Navy Advisory Group.
**Place and date:**
Republic of Vietnam, 31 October 1972.
**Entered service at:**
Spartanburg, S.C.
**Born:**
23 October 1949, Greenville, S.C.

**Citation:**
For conspicuous gallantry and intrepidity at the risk of his life above and beyond the call of duty while participating in a daring operation against enemy forces. PO Thornton, as Assistant U.S. Navy Advisor, along with a U.S. Navy lieutenant serving as Senior Advisor, accompanied a 3-man Vietnamese Navy

SEAL patrol on an intelligence gathering and prisoner capture operation against an enemy-occupied naval river base. Launched from a Vietnamese Navy junk in a rubber boat, the patrol reached land and was continuing on foot toward its objective when it suddenly came under heavy fire from a numerically superior force. The patrol called in naval gunfire support and then engaged the enemy in a fierce firefight, accounting for many enemy casualties before moving back to the waterline to prevent encirclement. Upon learning the senior advisor had been hit by enemy fire and was believed to be dead, PO Thornton returned through a hail of fire to the lieutenant's last position; quickly disposed of 2 enemy soldiers about to overrun the position, and succeeded in removing the seriously wounded and unconscious Senior Naval Advisor to the water's edge. He then inflated the lieutenant's lifejacket and towed him seaward for approximately 2 hours until picked up by support craft. By his extraordinary courage and perseverance, PO Thornton was directly responsible for saving the life of his superior officer and enabling the safe extraction of all patrol members, thereby upholding the highest traditions of the U.S. Naval Service.

## Thorsness, Leo K.

**Rank and organization:**
Lieutenant Colonel (then Maj.), U.S. Air Force, 357th Tactical Fighter Squadron.
**Place and date:**
Over North Vietnam, 19 April 1967.

**Entered service at:**
Walnut Grove, Minn.
**Born:**
14 February 1932, Walnut Grove, Minn.

**Citation:**
For conspicuous gallantry and intrepidity in action at the risk of his life above and beyond the call of duty. As pilot of an F-105 aircraft, Lt. Col. Thorsness was on a surface-to-air missile suppression mission over North Vietnam. Lt. Col. Thorsness and his wingman attacked and silenced a surface-to-air missile site with air-to-ground missiles, and then destroyed a second surface-to-air missile site with bombs. In the attack on the second missile site, Lt. Col. Thorsness' wingman was shot down by intensive antiaircraft fire, and the 2 crewmembers abandoned their aircraft. Lt. Col. Thorsness circled the descending parachutes to keep the crewmembers in sight and relay their position to the Search and Rescue Center. During this maneuver, a MIG-17 was sighted in the area. Lt. Col. Thorsness immediately initiated an attack and destroyed the MIG. Because his aircraft was low on fuel, he was forced to depart the area in search of a tanker. Upon being advised that 2 helicopters were orbiting over the downed crew's position and that there were hostile MIGs in the area posing a serious threat to the helicopters, Lt. Col. Thorsness, despite his low fuel conditions, decided to return alone through a hostile environment of surface-to-air missile and antiaircraft defenses to the downed crew's position.

As he approached the area, he spotted 4 MIG-17 aircraft and immediately initiated an attack on the MIGs, damaging 1 and driving the others away from the rescue scene. When it became apparent that an aircraft in the area was critically low on fuel and the crew would have to abandon the aircraft unless they could reach a tanker, Lt. Col. Thorsness, although critically short on fuel himself, helped to avert further possible loss of life and a friendly aircraft by recovering at a forward operating base, thus allowing the aircraft in emergency fuel condition to refuel safely. Lt. Col. Thorsness' extraordinary heroism, self-sacrifice, and personal bravery involving conspicuous risk of life were in the highest traditions of the military service, and have reflected great credit upon himself and the U.S. Air Force.

## Wetzel, Gary George

**Rank and organization:**
Specialist Fourth Class (then Pfc.), U.S. Army, 173d Assault Helicopter Company.
**Place and date:**
Near Ap Dong An, Republic of Vietnam, 8 January 1968.
**Entered service at:**
Milwaukee, Wis.
**Born:**
29 September 1947,
South Milwaukee, Wis.

**Citation:**
Sp4c. Wetzel, 173d Assault Helicopter Company, distinguished himself by conspicuous gallantry and intrepidity at the risk of his life, above and beyond the call of duty. Sp4c. Wetzel was serving as door gunner aboard a helicopter which was part of an insertion force trapped in a landing zone by intense and deadly hostile fire. Sp4c. Wetzel was going to the aid of his aircraft commander when he was blown into a rice paddy and critically wounded by 2 enemy rockets that exploded just inches from his location. Although bleeding profusely due to the loss of his left arm and severe wounds in his right arm, chest, and left leg, Sp4c. Wetzel staggered back to his original position in his gun well and took the enemy forces under fire. His machine-gun was the only weapon placing effective fire on the enemy at the time. Through a resolve that overcame the shock and intolerable pain of his injuries, Sp4c. Wetzel remained at his position until he had eliminated the automatic weapon emplacement that had been inflicting heavy casualties on the American troops and preventing them from moving against this strong enemy force. Refusing to attend his own extensive wounds, he attempted to return to the aid of his aircraft commander but passed out from loss of blood. Regaining consciousness, he persisted in his efforts to drag himself to the aid of his fellow crewman. After an agonizing effort, he came to the side of the crew chief who was attempting to drag the wounded aircraft commander to the safety of a nearby dike. Unswerving in his devotion to his fellow man, Sp4c. Wetzel assisted his crew chief even though he lost consciousness once again during this action. Sp4c. Wetzel displayed extraordinary heroisms in his efforts to aid his fellow crewman. His gallant actions were in keeping with the highest traditions of the U.S. Army and reflect great credit upon himself and the Armed Forces of his country.

## Williams, James E.

**Rank and organization:**
Boatswain's Mate First Class (PO1c.), U.S. Navy, River Section 531, My Tho, RVN.
**Place and date:**
Mekong River, Republic of Vietnam, 31 October 1966.
**Entered service at:**
Columbia, S.C.
**Born:**
13 June 1930, Rock Hill, S.C.

**Citation:**
For conspicuous gallantry and intrepidity at the risk of his life above and beyond the call of duty. PO1c. Williams was serving as Boat Captain and Patrol Officer aboard River Patrol Boat (PBR) 105 accompanied by another patrol boat

when the patrol was suddenly taken under fire by 2 enemy sampans. PO1c. Williams immediately ordered the fire returned, killing the crew of 1 enemy boat and causing the other sampan to take refuge in a nearby river inlet. Pursuing the fleeing sampan, the U.S. patrol encountered a heavy volume of small-arms fire from enemy forces, at close range, occupying well-concealed positions along the riverbank. Maneuvering through this fire, the patrol confronted a numerically superior enemy force aboard 2 enemy junks and 8 sampans augmented by heavy automatic weapons fire from ashore. In the savage battle that ensued, PO1c. Williams, with utter disregard for his safety exposed himself to the withering hail of enemy fire to direct counter-fire and inspire the actions of his patrol. Recognizing the overwhelming strength of the enemy force, PO1c. Williams deployed his patrol to await the arrival of armed helicopters. In the course of his movement he discovered an even larger concentration of enemy boats. Not waiting for the arrival of the armed helicopters, he displayed great initiative and boldly led the patrol through the intense enemy fire and damaged or destroyed 50 enemy sampans and 7 junks. This phase of the action completed, and with the arrival of the armed helicopters, PO1c. Williams directed the attack on the remaining enemy force. Now virtually dark, and although PO1c. Williams was aware that his boats would become even better targets, he ordered the patrol boats' search lights turned on to better illuminate the area and moved the patrol perilously close to shore to press the attack. Despite a waning supply of ammunition the patrol successfully engaged the enemy ashore and completed the rout of the enemy force. Under the leadership of PO1c. Williams, who demonstrated unusual professional skill and indomitable courage throughout the 3-hour battle, the patrol accounted for the destruction or loss of 65 enemy boats and inflicted numerous casualties on the enemy personnel. His extraordinary heroism and exemplary fighting spirit in the face of grave risks inspired the efforts of his men to defeat a larger enemy force, and are in keeping with the finest traditions of the U.S. Naval Service.